VOLCANOES:
Earth's Awakening

Text and photographs
by Katia and Maurice Krafft

Translated from the French
by Frances Frenaye

"Earth tells us more about ourselves
than any number of books. Because it re-
sists us. Man discovers himself when he
measures up to an obstacle."
(A. de Saint-Exupéry, *Wind, Sand and Stars*)

INCORPORATED
MAPLEWOOD, NEW JERSEY 07040

Originally published by Hachette Réalités
under the title *Volcans: Le reveil de la terre*

All the photographs in this book
were taken by Katia and Maurice Krafft
and are distributed by Explorer-Vulcain,
except p. 59: Lou Gwartney; pp. 64-65:
Gordon Harris; p. 66: Harry Gunkel; p. 73:
Jean-Jacques Bacquet; p. 76: Martin Mall;
p. 81: Jacques Fusilier; p. 158, 159 (#1):
Roger Werths (Woodfin Camp &
Associates); p. 159 (#2): Bill Thompson
(Woodfin Camp & Associates); p. 159 (#3):
Rayniak (Gamma/Liaison)

Our thanks also to our friend Roland Bénard
for having authorized our publication of
eight of his plates.

(*Note:* With the exception of such measures as
heights, depths, diameters, distances, pounds
and acres, which have been converted to the
English system, all measurements given are metric.)

Library of Congress Cataloging in Publication Data

Krafft, Katia.
 Volcanoes: earth's awakening.

 Translation of Volcans.
 Includes index.
 1. Volcanoes—Pictorial works. I. Krafft,
Maurice, joint author. II. Title.
QE522. K7213   551.2'1   80-19123
ISBN O-8437-3760-3
ISBN O-8437-3761-1 (deluxe)

Printed at Danner Press Corporation, Canton, Ohio, U.S.A.

Contents

Introduction

The progress that volcanology has made
since ancient scholars explained the lavas of
Vesuvius and Etna as products of combustion
and subterranean storms, is more apparent than real.
The sad fact is that we desperately need a coherent
and demonstrable theory of volcanism.
Why do volcanoes erupt?
The only honest answer is that we do not have the vaguest idea.

Alexander R. McBirney, volcanologist, 1976

The most grandiose, mysterious, and terrifying of all natural phenomena is that of a volcano in eruption. Trembling, cracking, roaring, smoking, exploding, surging, flowing, and disemboweling itself, it strikes terror into the heart of the beholder.

From the beginning of time man has been spellbound by this uncontrollable happening, one that defies human understanding. It has given rise to numberless beliefs, based on superstitious terror, fantastic legends, and hypotheses of the most extravagant kind.

4

The Roman poet Virgil attributed the eruptions of Etna to the desperate efforts of the rebellious Titan Enceladus to free himself from the underground prison to which Jupiter had consigned him. The trembling of the earth stemmed from his writhing, the eruption from his burning breath, and the rumbling from his plaintive voice. Moreover, the Greeks believed that their fire god, Hephaestus, frequented this vicinity. The Romans placed his dwelling in the crater of Vulcano in the Aeolian Islands, north of Sicily, and renamed him Vulcan. This unruly child of Jupiter and Juno, they said, had set up a forge beneath the crater, and there, amid flames and smoke, he hammered out the bronze arrows of Apollo, the impenetrable armor of Hercules, and the sculpted shield of Achilles. A temple dedicated to Vulcan, in the center of ancient Rome, celebrated every year (on August 23) the "Vulcanalia," in which propitiatory sacrifices were offered in order to ward off disasters from fire.

Mediterranean civilizations were not the first to embrace a volcano cult. Earlier societies had already made them objects of veneration. Primitive man could not but quail before the unleashed forces of nature and perceive in them a deity punishing their failure to render him due honor. There was a natural basis for the ancestral fear of obscure rumblings, flashes of light, smoke, red-hot lava, and dark landscapes buried under the remaining ash. Volcanic eruption could not but be proof of the anger of the gods at the deeds of mankind, provoking them to convert the divine gift of fire into a source of calamity.

The prehistoric hominids, or ape-men of eastern Africa, roamed around active volcanoes along the geological fault of this region three and a half million years ago. They may have discovered fire in the burning lava flowing down the wooded slope of a volcanic cone.

The primitive tribes of Tonga, in Polynesia, worshiped the hero Maui, a benevolent god who took fire from a volcano and gave it to man to warm his house and cook his food.

To the Maoris of New Zealand every eruption of Ngauruhoe signified a command to tribes in the region of Lake Taupo to wage war against their neighbors. Their account of the formation of the volcanoes and thermal zones of their native land is worth telling. One day Ngatoro, a magician from the island of Hawaiki (probably Hawaii), scaled the slopes of a volcano near Tongariro, along with Auruhoe, his favorite female slave. At the summit they were very cold, and Ngatoro begged his sisters to send him fire from the volcano of Hawaiki. His sorceress sisters called on demons who swam at feverish speed underwater toward New Zealand. At White Island they surfaced to take their bearings, and then plunged back into the water, leaving a volcano behind them. After reaching the mainland of New Zealand they journeyed underground, surfacing at intervals in the same manner and leaving hot springs of volcanoes, like so many molehills, along the way. Finally they arrived at Tongariro and gave Ngatoro the fire. But it was too late, for Auruhoe had already frozen to death. Her inconsolable master buried her in the crater, and from that day the volcano was called Ngauruhoe, a combination of their two names.

The goddess Pele is the most famous deity of the Pacific. She came from Tahiti, whence a quarrel with her sister, Namakaokahai, forced her into exile in the Halemaumau, the crater of the Kilauea volcano in Hawaii. She provokes all the volcanic activities of this island; in moments of anger she kicks open a crater with her heel and spills floods of lava onto her detractors. She appears, before every eruption, in the guise of a wrinkled old woman or, less often, that of a beautiful young girl. Innumerable legends of all kinds center around Pele, often attached to actual volcanic eruptions. Thus, one day, a chief from the eastern part of Hawaii was coasting on his *holua* (sled) down a grassy slope near his village. An old woman appeared to him and asked if she

*Popocatepetl in eruption
(from a 16th-century Mexican
manuscript)*

could borrow his sled. He refused, but a few minutes later she reappeared with another sled and proposed a race between them. He accepted the challenge and won the race. Angrily, she tapped the ground with her heel. It opened up, spat steam and ejected burning lava. Plainly the work of the goddess Pele! The young man made for the coast pursued by a rain of burning stones thrown by the enraged goddess. Fortunately, he managed to escape in a canoe. But even today we can see the hillside where he was coasting. It is marked by a row of cones, surrounded by volcanic slag, which testifies to an eruption such as that indicated in the legend.

Belief in Pele's supernatural powers lasted until the nineteenth century, when Kapiolani, the Christian wife of the chief of the Kona district, attempted to convert the people to her religion. In December of 1824 she undertook to show the tribe that Pele was no more than a myth. In spite of the efforts of her husband and friends to dissuade her, she set out on foot for Pele's dwelling. The way was long, and everyone she met discouraged her, but she tirelessly insisted: "If Pele kills me, then you can continue to worship her; otherwise you must turn to Holy Scripture." When she came to the edge of the volcano she broke with an ancient taboo, picking and eating some *ohelo* berries without offering any to the goddess. She threw stones into the crater of Kilauea and then descended to the edge of the lava lake, thereby piling desecration upon desecration. Pele gave no sign of life, and the Hawaiians, including even the goddess's high priest, were baptized.

A few people, however, clung to their superstition. In August of 1881, when lava from Mauna Loa threatened the town of Hilo, Princess Keelikoani, one of the last priestesses of the cult, faced up to the advancing flow, uttered spells and incantations, offered silk scarves, and emptied a bottle of brandy onto the flames. The next day the river halted. Again, in 1955, when a forked tongue of lava was moving toward Kapoho, the villagers offered songs, food, and tobacco to Pele, and the lava flow halted.

*A major 18th-century volcanic
eruption in Guatemala (photo
Bibliothèque Nationale)*

GUATIMALA

The offering of gifts as an act of worship and of appeasement of the volcanic deity's lust for power is found in many civilizations. In sixteenth-century Mexico, every October, the Indians living at the foot of the slag cone of Xitle (home of the goddess of the same name) used a cornmeal paste to make reproductions of volcanoes. Every house had an altar decked with conical "cakes," each one topped by a head, complete with eyes, wearing a paper costume and surrounded by offerings. After three weeks these idols were decapitated and eaten. The faithful believed that thus, through the magic power of the paste, the goddess Xitle entered into the bodies of every communicant. When the Spaniards came upon this cult they climbed the mountain, thereby profaning it in the terrified Indians' eyes, and found the interior of the crater filled with snakes, guardians of the goddess. The Indians told them that one day a priest had defied her to displace the lake lying at the foot of Xitle. The lake stayed where it was, and the priest enjoined the people to forsake the virtuous life which she had taught them and to give themselves over to dissipation. The goddess's anger was terrible indeed. Xitle began to erupt and ejected a huge quantity of lava which destroyed the outlying villages and swallowed up the pyramid of Cuicuilco, an event which actually took place when the volcano gave its last sign of life, in A.D. 76.

In Nicaragua the Coseguina volcano was thought to remain inactive only if every twenty-five years a baby was tossed into it. When the Spaniards arrived, many holocausts were still carried out by the Indians in the crater of Masaya. In order to propitiate the gods they threw dozens of virgins into the giant's maw.

Even today Bromo, in eastern Java, is a volcano with a sacred character. At the yearly feast of Kesodo five thousand people, led by priests, climb the slopes and walk in procession three times around the crater, tossing in coins, fruits, flowers, and live chickens in order to secure the gods' goodwill and the inactivity of the volcano during the coming year.

In Bali, not far away, the two sacred volcanoes of Agung and Batur, refuges of the Hindu deities expelled by the Moslems from Java, are objects of a fervent cult celebrated in dozens of temples. In 1971, when we visited the active cone of Batur, priests said to us: "We shall make offerings on your behalf to Siva, because by penetrating the crater you risk arousing his irritation."

In Japan, every year, hundreds of thousands of believers bow down and meditate before the famous Fujiyama or around the great cauldron of Aso San. Lonely old men, bankrupt businessmen, and jilted lovers, seeking an end to their woes, throw themselves into the crater of Mihara Yama.

There are abundant references to volcanoes in the Judeo-Christian tradition. Mount Sinai was an active volcano, and Yahweh strangely resembles a volcanic deity when we read: "Out of his nostrils goeth smoke . . . and a flame goeth out of his mouth" (Job 41: 6–7). Whereas God is endowed with a volcanic aspect, demons are not. The ancient Hebrews knew nothing of Satan's domain, which was the creation of the Church Fathers in the second century, when volcanoes were considered to be the entrances to hell. In the Middle Ages volcanic eruptions were interpreted as infernal fires and their rumbling as the complaint of the damned. Around 1600, Caspar Peucer wrote, on the subject of Iceland's Hekla volcano: "From the bottomless abyss of Hekla there issue forth sad sobs and hoarse groans which can be heard for miles around. . . . Here we have a shaft reaching down all the way to hell, and whenever there is a war anywhere on earth we hear weeping, wailing, and gnashing of teeth from deep under the mountain." Even today a Norseman may curse you by saying: "Go to Hekla!"

In the tenth century Icelanders regarded volcanic eruptions as natural phenomena, although their legends still spoke of the giant Loge (Loki), symbol of devouring flame, and Surtur, the Nordic god of fire. The latter's name was given to Surtsey, the new volcanic island which rose out of the sea in 1963 in the waters south of Iceland. As early as the year 1000, doubts were expressed concerning the existence of the pagan deities. In that year the Althing, the world's first democratic parliament, set up by the Vikings seventy years before, met at the edge of the flaw of Almannagia, on the "rock of the law," a site endowed with unusual acoustic qualities in the plain of Thingvellir, an expanse of hardened lava. The question to be debated was whether Iceland should embrace the Christian religion or continue to worship its old Nordic gods. Both solutions were expounded and bolstered by many arguments, and there seemed to be no way of reconciling the differences between them. The debate grew heated, and each side declared the other outside the law. At this moment a messenger arrived with the news that lava was gushing forth from a fissure at Aulfus, some eighteen miles to the east of Reykjavík, and threatening the village of Chief Thorodd. "You see," the pagans exclaimed, "the gods are vexed by your proposals." But Chief Snorre, a Christian, turned the news to his advantage. Pointing to the stretch of hardened lava on the plain around them, he asked: "And what vexed the gods at the time of this flow?" The pagans had no answer, and the saga tells that the subsequent vote was in favor of Christianity.

Unfortunately, certain volcanic eruptions have more than mythological connotations; they have laid waste great cities and entire regions, and killed thousands of people:

—Vesuvius (Italy), A.D. 79: two thousand deaths; Pompeii, Herculaneum, and Stabiae wiped off the map of the Roman Empire.

—Merapi (Indonesia), 1006: thousands of deaths; destruction of the empire of Mataram.

—Laki (Iceland), 1783: ten thousand people (25 percent of the island's population) starved to death.

—Tambora (Indonesia), 1815: ninety-two thousand deaths, of which eighty-two thousand were from starvation; destruction of two islands.

—Krakatau (Indonesia), 1883: thirty-six thousand deaths caused by the resultant tidal wave.

—Pelée (Martinique), 1902: twenty-eight thousand deaths; destruction of the town of Saint-Pierre.

But there was one eruption greater than all the others, four times more powerful than that of Krakatau, releasing energy equal to five million atomic bombs of the type dropped on Hiroshima and causing the decline of a whole civilization. It was the cataclysm that took place at Santorin, Greece, in 1500 B.C.

Santorin: Atlantis rediscovered or the end of the world

Santorin is an enormous horseshoe-shaped volcano in the center of the archipelago of the Cyclades, washed by the Aegean Sea. The crater (*caldera*) is nearly seven miles long, over four miles wide, and its one thousand nine-hundred-fifty-foot depth is filled with water. In the middle of this circular formation, bordered by cliffs made of many-colored layers of rock, there are two small islands covered with cones and fields of hardened lava. This Cyclopean setting was the scene, about fifteen hundred years before Christ, of one of the greatest volcanic disasters in all history, to which the size of the crater and the one hundred sixty-foot-thick layer of pumice covering all of the archipelago bear witness. Here is how, on the basis of studies made by archaeologists and volcanologists at both Santorin and Crete, it is possible to reconstruct the cataclysm.

In 1500 B.C. Santorin was a volcanic cone over three thousand feet high, topped by a small crater. On its slopes lived a peaceful community of prosperous merchants and artisans; it was one of the marketplaces of the Minoan world and the seat of the oldest and most refined civilization of the whole

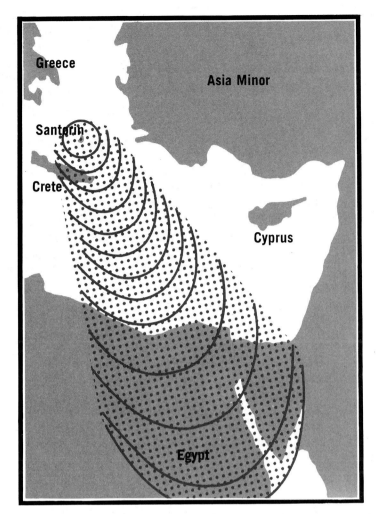

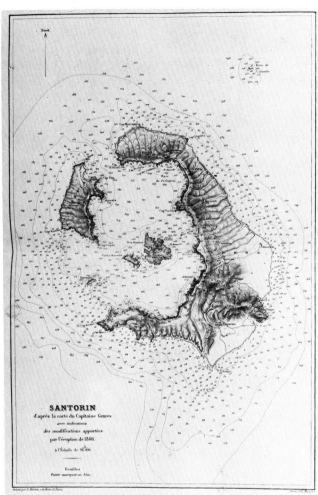

Aegean. Crete was its mother country, Knossos its capital. An all-powerful priest-king ruled this rich and prosperous state. Its people were orderly, delighting in bullfights, athletic contests and works of art, wearing elegant clothes and enjoying a freedom and social equality unusual in ancient times. From this base they sailed the Mediterranean in search of new trade outlets. In short, they lived in the best of all possible worlds.

Around 1580 B.C. an earthquake shook the whole region, partially destroying the famous Cretan temple of Knossos, but the Minoans quickly forgot about it. Eighty years later, the inhabitants of Santorin felt some tremors, but they were not unduly alarmed. As the tremors became more frequent the people began to question their meaning. Offerings were made to the gods, and a few families left the island. But the majority of the people were not disturbed. It was common knowledge that the Minoan region was subject to earthquakes. Little did they realize that their island was a special case.

One day shepherds brought word that the ground on the mountain slopes was hot under their feet and giving off a nauseous smell. A few weeks later there was a sudden and increasing motion. The walls of four-story houses of Akrotiri were rent, and barnyard animals were stricken with panic. The gods had spoken! Now people knew they must go. Gathering their most valuable belongings together, they fled to the shore. Their frail boats were weighed down almost to water level; some sank, but most of them stayed afloat and made their way south toward the mainland of Crete.

Soon after their departure the earthquake unleashed its full force. The ground opened up, walls cracked, roofs and columns tumbled, thousands of houses collapsed, and last-minute fugitives were killed by falling stones. The towns of Santorin lay in ruins. The reverberations of the quake were felt even in Knossos. Meanwhile the first boat people landed at Amnisos, the chief port of Crete, and told their story. The priest-king was informed and help was rushed to the refugees. A year went by. The refugees had trouble adapting themselves to a new life. They felt like provincials who had no place among the mainlanders. Fishermen brought news that calm had returned to Santorin, that the gods' anger was appeased. The refugees succumbed to the temptation to return. They rebuilt their houses, paved the streets, tilled the fields and resumed their everyday life. But there was fear in their hearts and they looked up nervously at the summit of the volcano. One night they saw bluish flames. The temperature of the smoke holes had risen, and sulphur was burning. The next morning the sky was clear, but for the first time a wreath of pure white smoke surrounded the summit. Later, larger and larger mushrooms of yellowish ash rose, with increasing din, into the air, and a rain of pumice powdered the town of Akrotiri. The people stopped short in their work as the ground began to tremble. The volcano had reawakened! With a feeling of death in their hearts they fled, taking with them, this time, all their worldly goods, because they knew that they would never return. Only heavy pots and vases, and the wall frescoes, were left behind. The rumbling noise became unbearable, and the air too dense to breathe. The sun was hidden behind the volcanic cloud, which spread out like an umbrella pine. The rain of pumice became thicker and thicker; it crackled on the rooftops, piled up in the streets and was burning to the touch. The recently rebuilt houses crumbled under the weight of volcanic dust. The people panicked. They ran, helter-skelter, to the boats. The sea was already covered with a coating of pumice, which delayed the boats, completely blocking some of them. A few were even sunk by a rain of stones and ash. Some people were asphyxiated or crushed, and then drowned, but most of them got away successfully. That evening, from afar, across the dusty water, they looked back, haggardly, at the incandescent stones crisscrossing and ricocheting in the air, then rolling down the slopes, leaving a fiery trail behind them. The arc of the horizon was red, and the air quivered with detonations. Subsequently Santorin was hidden from view by a curtain of black ash. An enormous dark column, shot through with flashes of light, rose up, accompanied by deafening explosions, over fifty miles into the air, while a deluge of rocks, pumice, and ash fell upon the island. Would-be scavengers, wandering among the ghost towns, were buried alive; birds were felled in their flight. Blazing fire, layers of lava and mud rolled over the area, burst through the house doors, filled the rooms and poured out through the windows, continuing their blind course until everything was submerged. Santorin was covered with a one hundred sixty-foot-thick shroud of pumice, which created an end-of-the-world landscape. The racket of the explosions could be heard in Crete, some seventy miles away, where terrified men hurried to make sacrifices to the gods in their sanctuaries. A great cloud obscured the horizon and shut out the sun. Slowly, but jerkily, the sea withdrew from the Cretan coast; the port towns of Mochlos, Nirou, and Amnisos were left high and dry. But after a short time a great tidal wave, three hundred feet high, descended upon the northern shore, sweeping away towns and villages, huts and palaces, drowning thousands of people and destroying the famous Minoan fleet, of which some vessels were swept far into the interior. Total darkness made for total confusion. A rain of fine white ash fell from the sky, blinding eyes and stopping up nostrils, penetrating houses and polluting the air. In the eastern part of Crete five inches of ash covered the ground; tree branches were broken, and torrents of mud flooded the valleys. Volcanic dust fell even as far away as Egypt.

Two days later, when the sun shone again over the Aegean, the volcano of Santorin had lost its majestic pointed cone. It had been decapitated and replaced by an immense crater with a capacity of almost seventy cubic kilometers, largely filled with seawater. Although the cataclysm was of a single day's duration, for weeks the surrounding sea was covered with a layer of pumice so thick that a man could walk upon it, and navigation was impossible. In Crete the harvest was destroyed, livestock died from the fluoride in the ash, and in the eastern region the water was undrinkable. Famine threatened but, in the long run, was staved off. From time to time a collapse in the interior of the crater gave rise to minor tidal waves which beat against the coast but found nothing left to destroy. With the spring, hope was reborn, vegetation pushed up through the ash, and water was again drinkable. But the Cretans remained apprehensive. If the gods had so harshly punished the inhabitants of Santorin, might not their turn be next? Their dynamic energy flagged, and they lost confidence in their invincibility.

A generation went by before there were more quakes, this time destroying the city of Zakros. Such was the impact of this renewed catastrophe that the Cretans turned against their priest-king. The realm was in disorder, and many of the people emigrated. With the eclipse of Crete's sea power, its hereditary enemy, Mycenae, gained control of the Aegean, invading and conquering its rival.

This cataclysm, destroyer of the Minoan world, is the source of numerous legends. It is interesting to note that Cretan civilization closely resembled that of the Atlantis described in Plato's *Crito* and *Timaeus*. There are the same magnificent palaces, the same social structure and addiction to bullfights. Plato wrote: "In the space of a day and night the army was swallowed up and the island of Atlantis sank into the sea." Archaeologists and geologists have recently shown that, if Atlantis really existed, we must look for it at Santorin and Crete. The flood of Deucalion, whereby Poseidon, god of the sea, revenged himself on Zeus by inundating Attica, Argolis, the Gulf of Salonika, Rhodes, and all the Mediterranean shores from Laodicea to Sicily, is probably a mythical description of the damage caused by the eruption of Santorin.

In another myth, when the Argonauts are preparing to cast anchor off Crete, Thalos, a bronze giant, throws slabs of rock at them; but Medea overcomes the monster, "whose blood runs like molten lead and who falls with a loud, cracking sound." The conquering Argonauts sail away, but "a terrible veil darkens the sea." The slabs of rock, the molten lead, the cracking sound, and the veil darkening the sea all seem to refer to the explosion, the earthquake, the lava flow, and the falling ash of Santorin.

The plagues visited upon Egypt and Moses' passage through the Red Sea (a lagoon bordering on the Mediterranean) may also be explained in the context of the same cataclysm.

In *Exodus*, the "darkness which may be felt" could have been caused by falling ash; the "waters . . . turned to blood," by the wealth of rust-red iron oxide in the volcanic dust which fell into the rivers; the "thunder," by the flashes of static electricity produced by friction among the ash; the "hail," by the crystallization of ice around the volcanic particles; the "frogs," by the tornadoes following upon the eruption which, as they passed over lakes, sucked up frogs along with water; the "death of the first-born" and the "ulcers" (boils), by the famine which followed upon the destruction of the harvest and the pollution of the water after volcanic ash had fallen upon them. Similarly, the proliferation of flies and the pestilence visited upon livestock may be connected with the rotting corpses of animals which had died of starvation. And, finally, lice and locusts may be said to have taken advantage of the destruction of the frogs, fish, and birds, killed by polluted water, which had habitually preyed upon them.

Moses and the Jews crossed the Red Sea at the moment when its waters withdrew before returning, an hour later, in the form of a tidal wave which swallowed up the pursuing Egyptian Army. We have no proof of a connection between the biblical story and the myths centering around the eruption of

Santorin. But there are cogent reasons for such a link. Admittedly, there is no scientific basis, for here we are in the realm of mythology.

Volcanic science: from subterranean winds to Plutonism

One of the earliest scientific approaches to the question of volcanoes was that of Plato (427?-347 B.C.). He claimed that earthquakes were caused by hot winds imprisoned and under pressure in immense subterranean caverns. They caught fire from contact with the great burning river, the Pyriphlegathon, and then gave birth to a volcano.

Within the same period Empedocles (fifth century B.C.), the philosopher of Agrigento in Sicily, went to study the mystery of Mount Etna and died there, engulfed by the yawning abyss. Legend has it that, when he became aware of his approaching end and wanted to be deified, he threw himself into the crater—which rejected him, spewing up his sandals.

Five centuries later, Strabo (63 B.C.-A.D. 30) said the volcanoes were giant safety valves, guaranteeing the life of the planet, an idea much in advance of his time. He was the first to recognize the volcanic nature of Vesuvius, previously considered an ordinary mountain. For Seneca (2 B.C.-A.D. 65) volcanoes were vents through which the melted matter of subterranean reservoirs arrived at the earth's surface. He, too, was a forerunner, for contemporary theory says much the same thing.

But the first real volcanologist was Pliny the Younger, whose letters to Tacitus give a faithful, detailed, almost scientific account of the eruption of Vesuvius in A.D. 79:

> *A cloud appeared, reminiscent in its shape of a tree, more exactly a pine . . . Ash fell . . . there was a rain of pumice and blackened pebbles, burned and pulverized by the fire . . . At this moment, on the summit, there were tongues and columns of flame, whose redness was accentuated by the darkness of the night . . . Houses were shaken by intense and repeated trembling of the earth . . . which seemed to push the sea away from the shore . . . The darkness of the night was blacker than that of any other . . . Behind us there was a terrifying dark cloud, shot through by the curving trajectories of twisting incandescent vapors. It opened from time to time as if to liberate great trains of fire . . . Women groaned, babies cried, men called out to their fathers, mothers, wives and children, trying to distinguish the voices with which they made reply. Some wept over their own misfortune, some over that of others, while some, in the moment of their agony, invoked death.*

After this we have sixteen centuries of silence, for it was not until the late Renaissance that there was a renewal of the scientific observation of volcanoes. Sometime around 1700 the French chemist Lémery noticed that a mixture of iron filings and flowers of sulphur, dampened by water, spontaneously heats up to the point of incandescence and gives off steam and other projected matter. This phenomenon, in his view, explained how sulphur ferments in the depths of the earth, causing both earthquakes and the conflagrations called volcanoes. The idea took root that volcanoes are produced by the combustion and fermentation of certain matter in contact with air and water. The famous French naturalist Buffon enthusiastically adopted this theory in his *Natural History*, written in the middle of the eighteenth century, where his detailed explanation runs in part as follows:

> *A volcano is an immense cannon whose barrel may be a mile in diameter. Its mouth vomits torrents of smoke and flames, rivers of bitumen, sulphur and molten metal, clouds of ash and stones . . . The noise, fire and smoke are caused by the fact that in the burning mountains there are accumulations of sulphur, bitumen and other flammable matter, as well as minerals and pyrites*

which ferment when exposed to air and dampness. When they catch fire there is an explosion proportional to the quantity of flammable matter . . . The center of volcanic activity is not deep down in the earth but near the surface; only for this reason does wind fan the combustion . . . This is a physicist's idea of a volcano . . .

This theory came to be known as "Neptunism" (from Neptune, god of the sea). Its prime exponent was Gottlob Werner, an authoritative professor of geology in the University of Freiberg, who strenuously maintained that all volcanic rocks, basalt included, were formed by the crystallization and sedimentation of a watery solution. Volcanic eruptions—rare and insignificant—were to be ascribed, in his view, to burning coal, which melted the rocks around it. As for the heat necessary for igniting the coal, it came from the effect of water on pyrite. Gottlob, it seems, had never seen a volcanic eruption, or he would not have propounded such stupidities. And yet, at the beginning of his career, he was an inspector of the foundries of Saxony, where every day he could observe the "volcanic" fusion of the blast furnaces.

An opposing theory, called "Plutonism" (from Pluto, god of Hades), soon emerged, under the leadership of an Englishman, James Hutton. His teachings were not new. They were based on the idea that the depths of the earth are in a state of permanent fusion and that through faults or fractures of the

surface, molten matter rises up and gives birth to a volcano. According to the Plutonists, basalt is definitely of volcanic origin. Despite their strong arguments, it took them seventy years to discredit the Neptunists.

In 1752 there occurred an event favorable to Plutonism. In a work entitled *Sur quelques montagnes de France qui ont été des volcans*, Jean-Étienne Guettard recognized the volcanic origin of the chain of *Puys*, the conical mountains in the region of Auvergne. "At a time when the Earth seems to be

A flood of lava advancing on an inhabited area during an 18th-century eruption of Vesuvius (photo Lalance)

in a state of ferment," he wrote, "it may be good to hear that many centuries ago this kingdom had volcanoes which might, at the slightest movement or provocation, be rekindled." He went on, unfortunately, to say: "Basalt is a kind of vitrified rock, formed by crystallization in a watery fluid, and there is no reason to consider it due to fusion by fire." Indeed, he said that columnar basalt is made of large crystals subjected to dissolution in water.

But in 1770 Nicolas Desmaret, after a visit to Auvergne, declared that the Puy de Dôme is an enormous granite block, heated on the spot by subterranean fire, and that basalt (and, hence, columnar basalt) has an igneous origin. Leopold von Buch was to declare that the Puy de Dôme is hollow, like a balloon, and that volcanic cones are shaped by the swelling of horizontal layers, raised up by deep-lying molten masses.

All the foregoing theories had their attractions, but it was high time that scientists who had actually observed volcanic eruptions should have their say. Sir William Hamilton, British ambassador to the Kingdom of Naples, published in 1774 a well-documented account of eruptions of both Vesuvius and Etna. In the same decade Lazzaro Spallanzani gathered rocks from the volcanic island of Stromboli and melted them down in order to analyze their composition and gas content. Later, Gratet de Dolomieu visited various Italian volcanoes, made the first mineralogical study of lava, and pinned down the igneous and volcanic origin of basalt.

At the same time, perversely enough, Scipione Breislak proposed a totally fantastic explanation of the eruptions of Vesuvius. The pyritic coal of the Ap-

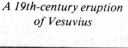
A 19th-century eruption of Vesuvius

How affluent tourists climbed
the slopes of Vesuvius at the
beginning of the 20th century

ennines, he said, underwent a subterranean distillation which gave rise to oil. This oil filtered its way southward and came to rest floating on the sea-water contained by the crater. When an electrical discharge, such as light-ning, took place, the oil caught fire and produced an eruption. Bernardin de Saint-Pierre, author of *Paul et Virginie*, held an even more wildly imagina-tive theory. Volcanoes, he said, are huge furnaces ignited around the oceans in order to purge their waters of pollution.

Only in the mid-nineteenth century did the first study of volcanic rock under a polarizing microscope and the creation of a volcanological laboratory at Vesuvius lead to the definitive triumph of Plutonism and the rudiments of the science of volcanology. Finally there evolved a satisfactory definition of a volcano: a natural apparatus by which the earth's crust is put into temporary or permanent communication with the molten matter of its interior. Erup-tions bear witness, gases are the motors, and molten rock the vehicle.

The real beginning of scientific volcanology took place in 1902. On May 8 of that year, on the Caribbean island of Martinique, a huge incandescent avalanche rolled out of the crater of Mount Pelée, destroying everything in its path, including the twenty-eight thousand inhabitants of the city of Saint-Pierre. Two geologists were summoned to the scene—the Frenchman Alfred Lacroix and the American Thomas Jaggar. Deeply impressed by this experi-ence, they went on to become the greatest volcanologists of the twentieth cen-tury. Lacroix won fame by his important studies of the petrography and mineralogy of volcanoes; Jaggar, by his works on the dynamism of volcanic eruptions and the method of predicting their occurrence. Here is how Jaggar tells us of the birth of his vocation: "As I look back on the Martinique expedi-tion, I know what a crucial point in my life it was and that it was the human

Modern volcanology born amid the ruins of Saint-Pierre in Martinique

contacts, not field adventure, which inspired me. Gradually I realized that the killing of thousands of persons by subterranean machinery totally unknown to geologists, and then unexplainable, was worthy of a life's work." In 1912 he founded the volcanological observatory of Hawaii, dedicated to the study of the volcanoes of Kilauea and Mauna Loa. He realized that understanding of the mechanism of volcanoes and predictions of their eruption entailed various sciences: seismology, geochemistry, physics, mineralogy, petrography, tectonics, and stratigraphy. All of these disciplines he drew on. Using measuring instruments, often of his own invention, to study the Hawaiian volcanoes, he was able to detect the first warnings of a crisis. Before erupting, a volcano displays three symptoms: tremors, swelling, and increased temperature.

Jaggar's observations bore fruit. At the beginning of 1935 he noticed that the earth was trembling and rumbling some thirty-five miles beneath Mauna Loa. These disturbances were mounting toward the surface at the rate of several hundred yards a day, together with a rising body of lava which, like a wedge, tore open and penetrated every fissure and proceeded, jerkily, toward the point of eruption. Jaggar announced that activity was imminent and that there would be a flow of lava toward the town of Hilo. On November 21, 1935, this is exactly what took place, marking the first accurate prediction of a volcanic eruption.

In 1942 Jaggar's former pupil and successor, R. H. Finch, renewed this achievement—thanks, in part, to immediately preceding earthquakes but also to the topographical alterations which preceded the eruption. The mounting molten rock came to occupy more and more space at the top of the volcanic mountain, puffing it up considerably. On March 28, Finch said that in the following week there would be activity on the northeast slopes of Mauna Loa, at an altitude between 10,800 and 11,800 feet. Activity began in the anticipated area and at an altitude of 11,150 feet. More recently (5:45 p.m., November 10, 1973), while five hundred tourists were admiring the lava lake of Mauna Ulu on Kilauea, volcanologists registered a rapid crumbling of the volcano's summit. They concluded that magma was making its way toward one side of the mountain and would burst forth across the road to the lava lake, thereby cutting off the tourists. As a result, the tourists were quickly evacuated. And, at 9:47 p.m., a fissure burst open and spilled lava onto the road.

Today there are more sophisticated techniques for predicting volcanic eruptions. Satellites, for instance, furnish data to volcanologists. Before erupting, a volcano heats up; the temperature of the fumaroles rises, and there are other thermal anomalies susceptible to satellite observation. In 1963 the activity of Surtsey, south of Iceland, did not escape the electronic eye of Nimbus II. The day before the volcano appeared above the sea, Nimbus recorded a hot point at the exact point in the Atlantic Ocean where the new island was to come into being.

Here we have seen successful predictions but, for two reasons, these remain exceptions. First, because although many volcanic eruptions have been observed, described and catalogued, we still do not understand why and how they take place. Second, because there are only some twenty observatories and about a hundred volcanologists to watch over the five hundred potentially active volcanoes of the planet, and there is no absolute assurance that the thousands of existing examples—including those of ancient times—are permanently extinct. Obviously, it would be too expensive to equip an observatory for every one of them. Iceland alone would require five hundred, and the expense would consume most of the national budget. It would be totally impractical for France to pay volcanologists to watch over the cones of Auvergne, which may not return to activity for another five or ten thousand years, if ever. It would be wiser to develop means of eliminating or lessening the damage caused by an unforeseen eruption. In Hawaii, in 1935 and 1942,

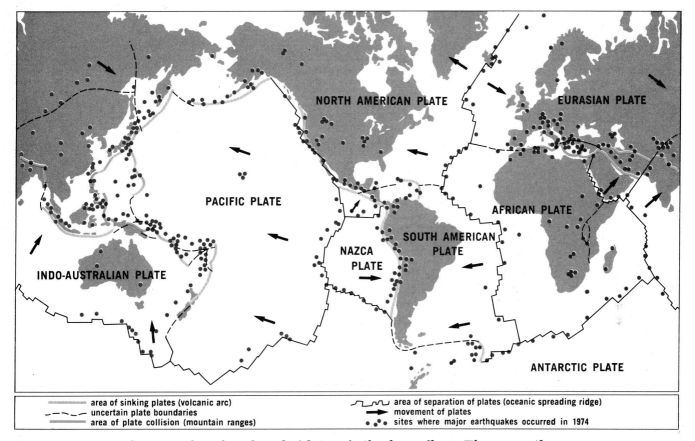

Jaggar sent airplanes to bombard and sidetrack the lava flow. These partly successful tactics constituted a real innovation. In 1973, when Mount Eldfell, on Heimaey island, south of Iceland, erupted, for weeks the local people poured four thousand cubic meters of seawater every hour onto the advancing stream of lava, arresting and hardening three thousand cubic meters of the flow per hour and saving their town from destruction.

A "new breed" of volcanologists is yet to come into being: experts on call for emergencies in any part of the globe, equipped to stem volcanic activity and save human lives. Unfortunately, volcanological studies are not well financed and their future possibilities depend on the damage wrought by the next eruption. Not that volcanoes are such terrible killers; in the last five hundred years they have caused the death of only two hundred thousand people, while four hundred thousand die every year in automobile accidents. Geologists long underestimated the importance of volcanoes, considering them natural curiosities of secondary importance. But in the light of contemporary theory they play a fundamental geological role in the evolution of the planet. They were involved in the origin of two thirds of the earth's surface, particularly of the ocean bottom, which is solid basalt. In the course of geological time millions of volcanoes have been active both above and under the sea. They bear witness to the vitality of the planet Earth and will not cease to spew forth their lava until billions of years from now, when it is dead. For the time being Earth breathes and lives through all the pores of its skin and the breaks in its crust, along the boundaries of a dozen puzzle pieces which float, like rafts or ice floes, over the underlying magma. Along these constantly shifting, scar-like conjunctions is strung out a chain of volcanoes.

Long life to the craters! Without them there would be no atmosphere and no water on the planet, no diamonds in South Africa, no thrice-yearly rice harvests on the island of Java; the central Italian railways would not run (as they do) on geothermal energy; tourists would not visit Pompeii. Yes, long life to them, in order that we may continue to admire the grandiose, mysterious, and fascinating anger inherent in a volcanic eruption!

The World: a puzzle made up of a dozen conjunctive puzzle pieces whose boundaries are marked by lines connecting one earthquake with another

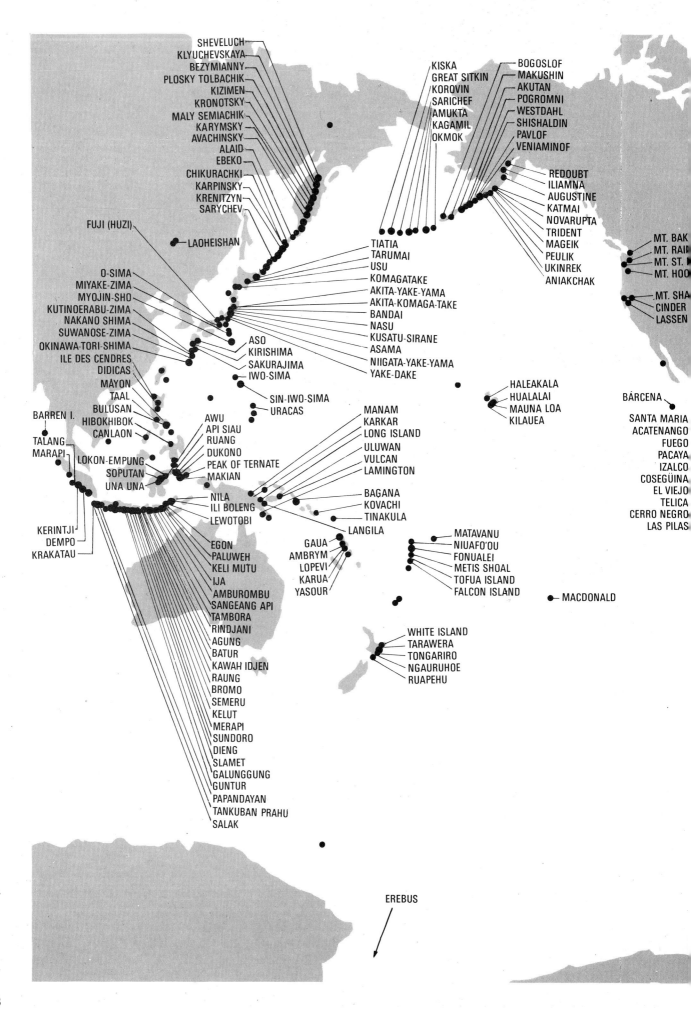

SHEVELUCH
KLYUCHEVSKAYA
BEZYMIANNY
PLOSKY TOLBACHIK
KIZIMEN
KRONOTSKY
MALY SEMIACHIK
KARYMSKY
AVACHINSKY
ALAID
EBEKO
CHIKURACHKI
KARPINSKY
KRENITZYN
SARYCHEV

FUJI (HUZI)
LAOHEISHAN

O-SIMA
MIYAKE-ZIMA
MYOJIN-SHO
KUTINOERABU-ZIMA
NAKANO SHIMA
SUWANOSE-ZIMA
OKINAWA-TORI-SHIMA
ILE DES CENDRES
DIDICAS
MAYON
TAAL
BULUSAN
HIBOKHIBOK
CANLAON

BARREN I.

TALANG
MARAPI

LOKON-EMPUNG
SOPUTAN
UNA UNA

KERINTJI
DEMPO
KRAKATAU

AWU
API SIAU
RUANG
DUKONO
PEAK OF TERNATE
MAKIAN

NILA
ILI BOLENG
LEWOTOBI

EGON
PALUWEH
KELI MUTU
IJA
AMBUROMBU
SANGEANG API
TAMBORA
RINDJANI
AGUNG
BATUR
KAWAH IDJEN
RAUNG
BROMO
SEMERU
KELUT
MERAPI
SUNDORO
DIENG
SLAMET
GALUNGGUNG
GUNTUR
PAPANDAYAN
TANKUBAN PRAHU
SALAK

TIATIA
TARUMAI
USU
KOMAGATAKE
AKITA-YAKE-YAMA
AKITA-KOMAGA-TAKE
BANDAI
NASU
KUSATU-SIRANE
ASAMA
NIIGATA-YAKE-YAMA
YAKE-DAKE

ASO
KIRISHIMA
SAKURAJIMA
IWO-SIMA

SIN-IWO-SIMA
URACAS

MANAM
KARKAR
LONG ISLAND
ULUWAN
VULCAN
LAMINGTON

BAGANA
KOVACHI
TINAKULA
LANGILA

GAUA
AMBRYM
LOPEVI
KARUA
YASOUR

KISKA
GREAT SITKIN
KOROVIN
SARICHEF
AMUKTA
KAGAMIL
OKMOK

BOGOSLOF
MAKUSHIN
AKUTAN
POGROMNI
WESTDAHL
SHISHALDIN
PAVLOF
VENIAMINOF

REDOUBT
ILIAMNA
AUGUSTINE
KATMAI
NOVARUPTA
TRIDENT
MAGEIK
PEULIK
UKINREK
ANIAKCHAK

MT. BAK
MT. RAI
MT. ST. I
MT. HOO

MT. SHA
CINDER
LASSEN

HALEAKALA
HUALALAI
MAUNA LOA
KILAUEA

BÁRCENA

SANTA MARIA
ACATENANGO
FUEGO
PACAYA
IZALCO
COSEGÜINA
EL VIEJO
TELICA
CERRO NEGRO
LAS PILAS

MATAVANU
NIUAFO'OU
FONUALEI
METIS SHOAL
TOFUA ISLAND
FALCON ISLAND

MACDONALD

WHITE ISLAND
TARAWERA
TONGARIRO
NGAURUHOE
RUAPEHU

EREBUS

Location of the world's principal active volcanoes

Sleeping monsters

Monsters for thousands of years asleep,
grumbling and stirring in their dreams, and waking
at intervals for a grandiose birth,
for violent combats in which puny, ant-like man
is only a powerless spectator.
At the four corners of the earth, from ice fields
all the way to the burning tropics, volcanoes engender
landscapes of all conceivable kinds . . .
Proud, slender cones, chimneys as rigid as ruins,
the gentle contours of ash-covered slopes, the harmonious curves
of craters, mysterious and diaphanous spirals,
icy lace laid over stretches of dark minerals . . .
Alternately fearsome and peaceful, destructive and benevolent,
these are volcanoes.

Page 21:
Seen through the branches of flowering almond trees, the snow-covered slopes of Mount Etna (Sicily), one of the world's most active volcanoes.

Pages 22–23:
Merapi, the "Mountain of Fire," on the island of Java (Indonesia), was, for a long time, the world's most regularly murderous volcano. During the paroxysm of 1006 it turned the center of Java into a sea of ash, wiping out the civilization of the Kingdom of Mataram. Today Indonesian volcanologists are at the monster's bedside, watching out for its fevers and palpitations. At the least tremor they advise evacuation of the many villages at the foot of the mountain.

Jewels in the Pacific's "Ring of Fire"

The same steep, symmetrical cones, the same sticky lava of andesitic origin, the same violently explosive eruptions characterize most of the volcanoes strung out along the "ring of fire" bordering the Pacific basin, from Indonesia to Japan and the Philippines, from South and Central America to the Aleutian Islands.

Whereas the fertile slopes of Merapi are heavily inhabited, those of the volcanoes of Alaska are empty, and their eruptions are no threat to human life . . .

1) Successive eruptions over millions of years have built up the "Pavlof family" of Alaska. It consists of the still active Pavlof (center), whose smoking crater regularly expels a trail of ash; Little Pavlof (foreground), long extinguished and diminished by erosion; and Pavlof Sister (rear), which erupts sporadically.

2) In its youth Aniakchak (Alaska) must have resembled the elegant Pavlof, but its summit was decapitated by an extremely violent explosion and replaced by a large crater (caldera). It has occasional periods of activity, such as occurred in 1931, responsible for the magnificent black and white stripes on the crater's slopes.

2

Life-giving steam and death-dealing gas

Old volcanoes and subsided craters exhale vapors and toxic gases, the last whiffs of their past activity. Under the thermal zones deep in the warm entrails of the earth, a reservoir of lava gives out heat. Rainwater seeps down, circulates in these depths, heats up and rises to the surface in the form of steam.

Page 26:
The area of Kawah Kamodjang (Indonesia), at 5,500 feet above sea level, would normally have scarce vegetation. Because of the heat and the wealth of carbonic acid gas surging up through the smoke holes of the volcano, it abounds in tropical flowers.

Page 27:
Around the Papandajan volcano (also in Indonesia) the contrary is true; we find desolation. From the cracked soil, with scattered ponds and puddles of burning mud, there rises a mixture of acid and corrosive gases which have destroyed the forests that formerly covered the slopes of the crater. Streams of hot, sulphurous water lay sticky black mud on the stones worn by the volcano. Animals, attracted by the sound of running water, lose their way in low-lying areas with stagnating layers of carbonic acid gas, carbon monoxide, and hydrogen sulphide. Trapped in these valleys of death, they are overpowered by asphyxiation.

Kilimanjaro: a birthday present to Kaiser Wilhelm II

At the end of the last century Kenya was ruled by Queen Victoria; and Tanzania (then Tanganyika), by Kaiser Wilhelm II of Germany, her grandson. For one of his birthdays the Queen offered him a truly imperial present: Kilimanjaro, the highest mountain in Africa, which, for this reason, is today in Tanzania. In 1848 a German missionary, John Rebmann, discovered what he called "a very high mountain covered with eternal snow." "Snow in the tropics? Impossible!" said pundits. But they had to give in to the evidence. After several climbers had failed to reach the top, in 1889 Hans Meyer, a German geographer, was successful.

1) In our day hundreds of tourists climb the volcano every year. On the third day of the ascent they come to this 5-mile-long desert plateau, which, at an altitude of 14,400 feet, separates the two summits: Mawenzi and Kibo (*in the background*). To the natives who live at the foot, Kibo has supernatural powers and contains treasures. It represents eternity, the immutable, and also divine kindness, for the rain from its clouds makes the soil fertile.

2) To geologists Kilimanjaro is an enormous stratovolcano resting on a base covering an area of 50 x 30 miles. It dates back to over a million years and has three centers of volcanic activity. These are, in order of age, Shira (13,143 feet), eroded to the point where it is a hilly plateau; Mawenzi (16,893 feet), dismantled, to a lesser extent, by erosion and resembling an ancient fortress; and Kibo (19,350 feet), a well-preserved cone surmounted by a mile-and-a-half-wide caldera containing two interlocking craters, 3,600 and 1,100 feet in diameter respectively. The smoke holes attain a temperature of 104° C, and abundant deposits of sulphur suggest that the last eruption was only a few centuries ago. Is the volcano extinct or simply sleeping? Only time will tell.

1

2

1

Mythical giants of Mexico

1) Like Kilimanjaro, the giant Popocatépetl, the "smoking mountain" in Nahuatl (17,887 feet) is a stratovolcano. Its comparatively recent cone, built on an older volcanic edifice 12,450 feet high, is topped by a crater with a 1,900-foot diameter and a small navel at the center. The cone is badly breached and covered with smoke holes and sulphur deposits. At the beginning of the 16th century, when the Spaniards conquered Mexico, Cortez dispatched an expedition to bring back sulphur with which to make gunpowder for his siege of Tenochtitlán. Aztec Indians were lowered into the crater in search of the sulphur deposits. Later conquistadors followed this example, and mountaineers known as *volcaneros* made a regular business of it. On February 19, 1919, a dynamiting operation inside the crater provoked tremors and collapses which caused the death of nineteen workers. A few months later a dome of viscous lava rose up and destroyed the entire operation.

Near Popocatépetl there is a defunct, flattened and eroded volcanic mountain, covered with snow, Iztaccihuatl, or "Recumbent Woman" (17,455 feet). Legend has it that Pocatépetl was in love with Iztaccihuatl. He went off to a long-lasting war and, when he came back, he found that his beloved had died of sorrow. He laid her out on top of a mountain to which he gave her name, covered her with a shroud of white snow and watched over her with a lighted torch. Eventually he died, but the torch (the smoke holes) is still burning.

2) Although Popocatépetl is Mexico's most famous volcano, Colima (12,992 feet), in the state of Jalisco, is the most active. Its steep cone settled itself into the hollow of an old caldera in the shadow of its "father," the eroded Nevado de Colima (14,173 feet). Colima is highly turbulent. At regular intervals it vomits a slow-moving viscous flow of lava and dark rock, spits ash in cauliflower formation or, occasionally, emits a glowing cloud, an incandescent emulsion which rolls down at lightning speed toward the plain below.

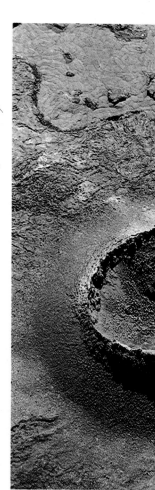

1

2

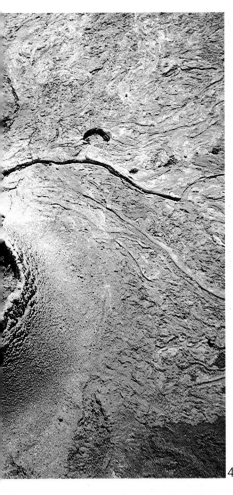

4

3

A universe of circles

The circle is the dominating form in the world of volcanoes. The matter which they eject distributes itself more or less uniformly around the outlet and shapes a cone surmounted by a crater. The more powerful the explosion, the more finely it shatters the lava, which volcanologists divide, according to decreasing size, into the following categories: blocks, bombs, scoriae, lapilli, and ash.

1) Longonot (Kenya), born a million years ago, is a majestic cone topped by a caldera a mile in diameter. After a long period of inactivity, during which erosion had carved innumerable ridges in its slopes, earning it the native name of "the mountain with many trails," a smaller crater, a sort of blister, erupted, at the end of the last century, on the side of its big sister.

2) All curves and rounded lines, this asymmetrical construction made of ash and lapilli, covered by greenery, has a diameter of only 1,300 feet and an altitude of only 300 feet. It came into being in the course of only a few days less than a thousand years ago, and is located between Lake Natron and the volcano of Ol Doinyo Lengai in Tanzania. This region is full of equally asymmetrical cones, whose northern wall is much higher than the others because the prevailing wind is from the south and, during periods of eruption, pushes the pro-jected matter in a northerly direction.

3) Because of its perfect shape .the Pariou (800 feet above sea level) is the jewel of the chain of *Puys* in central France. At the bottom of its 800-foot-wide and 300-foot-deep crater the members of the French Geological Society, wearing top hats and stiff collars, met on August 30, 1833. Born around eight thousand years ago, inside a caldera formed by an earlier eruption, this extinct volcano is often called "the French Vesuvius," because it, too, is formed of two interlocking constructions.

4) This crater of the Piton de la Fournaise (Réunion), only about 200 feet above sea level and with a base 500 feet in diameter, is very different from the three others just described. The ejected lava was so hot and fluid that the fragments of molten rock joined together as they fell and made a steep wall around the outlet. At the same time two lava lakes accumulated—one in the crater, the other in a depression at the foot of the cone. Later they emptied, as if a dam had given way, liberating floods of molten rock which instantly covered vast areas with bubbling basaltic dust. Every little lava pond left some trace of its existence—the first by breaching the crater, the second by forming a flat stretch covered by gray elephant skin (visible at the top of the illustration). The eruption, which began on November 15, 1972, came to an end on December 10 of the same year.

When a volcano lights street lights . . .

Mount Spurr (Alaska) had not erupted in the memory of man when suddenly, at 5 a.m. on July 9, 1953, on its southern flank, an ice-filled crater violently expelled a train of cinders, blocks, steam, and gases in the mushroom shape of an atomic explosion. The heavy spiral rose rapidly to a height of 65,000 feet. Toward noon volcanic ash fell on the 80-mile-distant city of Anchorage. The resulting darkness was such that it triggered the mechanism that turned on the street lights.

From Mount Spurr in the northeast to the undersea volcanic depression of Buldir in the southwest, along the 1,600-mile-long volcanic arc of Alaska and the Aleutian Islands, a chain of eighty active volcanoes forms a fiery girdle whose frosty summits pierce through a sea of white clouds.

1) Among them is Pavlof, whose icy robe is punctuated by ice-filled craters surmounted by steam.

2) These slender, steep cones watch over pastures of fleecy clouds. Shishaldin, the most perfectly shaped among them, rises majestically. Only Fujiyama and Mount Mayon in the Philippines can rival the elegance and symmetry of this Aleutian jewel. Because it rises from the uninhabited island of Unimak, usually shrouded in clouds, there are few witnesses to its eruptions. Sometimes airline pilots, when the clouds lift, observe that black ash has stained the snow, testifying to an awakening of the angry giant.

On a mysterious island bastion of the Moluccas a ghostly volcano emerges from a gray morning at Ternate (Indonesia).

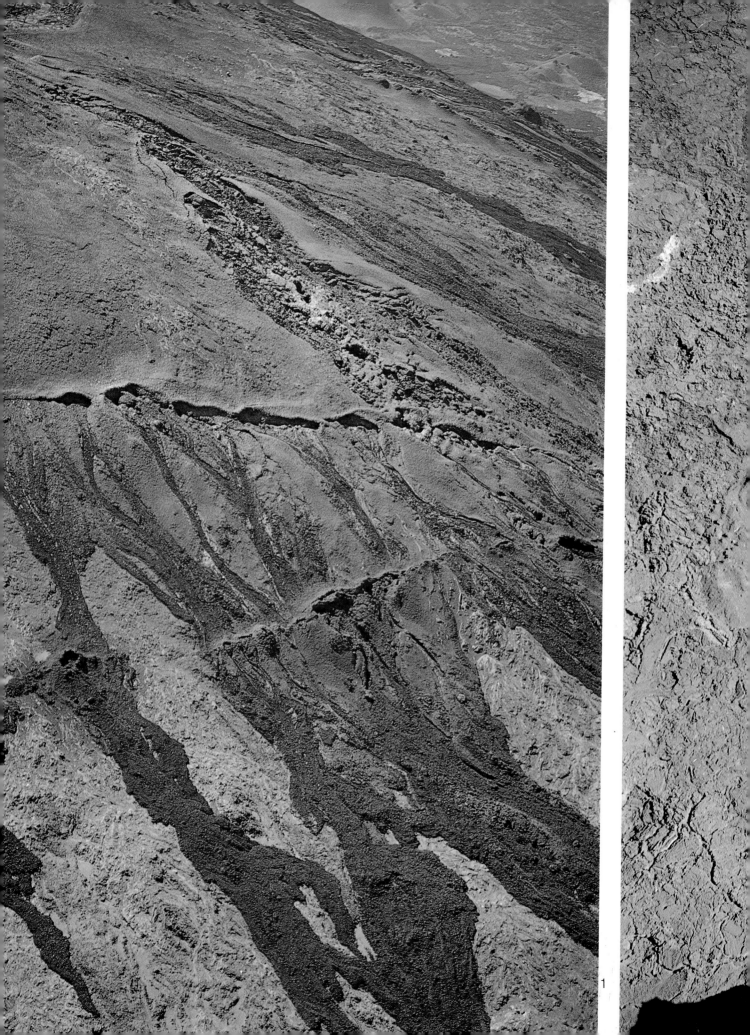

1

La Fournaise: the planet's most active volcano

It all began three million years ago, when a volcano was born on the floor of the Indian Ocean, 13,000 feet below the actual site of the island of La Réunion. The cone rose, little by little, until, a million years later, the Piton des Neiges (peak of snow) reached a height of 10,000 feet above sea level. Eruptions became more frequent, and, as a basalt structure built up, the island grew in diameter as well as in height, and the volcano turned into a gigantic flattened cone. A mere three hundred thousand years ago it changed its ways and became highly explosive, emitting incandescent ash clouds and subsequently flows of mud. At this juncture a small but turbulent volcano—the future Piton de la Fournaise—made its appearance. Like a wart it came out on the southeast side of the Piton des Neiges and grew until it was the equal of its elder brother, which became inactive thirty thousand years ago.

Today the Piton de la Fournaise is a magnificent basalt structure, 8,632 feet high, rent by two large-scale collapses of which the more recent, l'Enclos, measuring 7 by 4 miles, shelters a majestic cone, Le Bory, crowned by two craters. It is in l'Enclos, an uninhabited caldera, that, almost every year, there is a magnificent display of fireworks, which makes La Fournaise the most active volcano on the planet.

1) Fissures have split open a side of Le Bory, and for several hours lava has seeped out of it like blood from an open wound.

2) Often magma, rich in gases, wells up in fountains of incandescent lava which build partial cones like those of this strange small ant lion hole that appeared in 1964, flanked by a small gas outlet. Subsequent flows surrounded it, partially submerging another volcano, dating from 1963 (in the background), reddened by fumaroles.

Fire lurks under the ice

Contrary to what one might think, many volcanoes are buried under ice.

1) In Africa, Kilimanjaro's summit is covered by glaciers and year-round snow whose partial melting under the fiery equatorial sun produces strange, needle-like shapes known as the "ice penitents."

In Iceland such active volcanoes as Katla and Grimsvötn wear a thick, icy cap. Extremely violent eruptions occur when the molten lava comes in contact with the ice, powerful phreatic explosions break up rocks and ice fields, and great streams of mud, carrying with them ice, rocks, earth and ash, and destroying everything in their path as they rush at a speed of some 40 miles an hour down the valleys which radiate from the mountain's summit.

2) Almost all the volcanoes of Alaska are coated with snow and ice. This aerial view of Katmai Monument shows several important volcanic summits. In the foreground is Mount Mageik (7,136 feet), of which only the active crater is devoid of snow. At the bottom is an emerald-green lake, where many fumaroles fizzle. Every few years it throws up a train of ash. Behind it, separated by the Katmai saddle (col), is Young Trident, a black dome whose tentacles of viscous lava embrace a grayish cone. Its birth was announced on February 15, 1953, by the rise of a dark cloud, like an atomic mushroom which pushed itself up over 6 miles into the air. In the background is its snow-covered ancestor, Old Trident. In the distance, bordered by a steep cliff just in front of the chain of snowy mountains, is the caldera of Katmai, a product of the biggest eruption of the century, which, in 1912, created the Valley of Ten Thousand Smokes.

1

2

2

A refuge of the gods and a devil's cavern

1) The Ol Doinyo Lengai, or "Mountain of God" (Tanzania), in the Great Rift Valley of East Africa, is sacred to the tribes that live around it. Its steep slopes are carpeted with slippery, grayish ash and broken by deep ravines. Twin craters, like monstrous and sinister eyes sunk into their sockets, stare up at the sky. Ol Doinyo Lengai is baffling to volcanologists because it is the only volcano in the world that emits a calcareous flow, that is, lava made up of sodium and calcium carbonate. The latest eruption, in 1966, from the upper crater, was subjected to considerable scientific observation. To the amazement of the assembled volcanologists, the fountains of lava and the molten matter gushing from two small cones were black and not in the least incandescent. Only when they had cooled off did they turn white.

2) Over a thousand miles away, in the Republic of Djibouti, the Afar tribes have baptized the island shown above "Ginni Koma," or Devil's Island. There is nothing infernal about it; the name was given it, perhaps, because a remote ancestor of the Afars witnessed its terrible birth in a titanic combat between boiling lava and a raging sea. Its haystack profile, above a flat crater, and its ocher color are characteristic of an underwater formation. In the course of its existence Ginni Koma has been pushed up by movements of the ocean floor. Behind it are beds of black lava, scarred by fissures and punctuated by cones left by the sinking of Ardoukoba, when colossal forces ripped the earth's crust and separated Africa from Arabia. On November 7, 1978, volcanologists were amazed by the resurgence of a volcano after thousands of years of inactivity. The devil got himself once more into the news!

The Valley of
Ten Thousand Smokes:
The 20th century's
greatest eruption

On June 1, 1912, increasingly severe tremors shook the region of Katmai in Alaska and were felt more than a hundred miles away. The Eskimo inhabitants of the two nearest villages fled. About one o'clock in the afternoon of June 6 an explosion of unprecedented violence rent the air and was heard as far as Juneau, nearly 750 miles away. Further explosions followed at an increasingly rapid rate for two days. Quantities of pumice

and ash, interspersed with dazzling flashes of light, rose up and then showered down onto the ground. The darkness was such that at Kodiak, about 100 miles away, a lamp held at arm's length was not visible to the bearer. In this remote town panic reigned, for the static engendered by the friction of ash particles cut off radio communication. Pumice crackled on the rooftops and piled up in the streets. Houses crumpled un-

der the onslaught of this mineral snow and earthslides roared down the mountainsides. Many townspeople embarked on a freighter to escape, but the ship was immobilized by dust and darkness. Four days went by before the rain of ash ceased and a pallid light returned to the sky.

Only in 1916 did Robert Griggs and Lucius G. Folsom visit the site of the eruption. To their astonishment, the former riverbed of the Ukak River—

and, indeed, the whole of its broad valley—had become a hardened yellowish-orange mass, 12 miles long and 3 miles wide. Thousands upon thousands of pure, white fumaroles gushed, dancing and spiraling as high as a thousand feet into the air and giving rise to the name ''Valley of Ten Thousand Smokes.'' In a few hours, a forested green area, the home of bears and caribou, had been submerged by a layer of pumice and

burning ash, rich in gas, which has streamed, like milk spilling out of a pot, into the valley, and transformed it into a sea of mineral foam.

1 and 2) Today only occasional emanations of steam rise from the site of the enormous deposit. Rivers have redug their beds, carving out canyons which run through the golden-yellow shroud of the dead valley, whose jagged forms have been softened by time.

2

1

The guilty eye

Many expeditions will have to be made to the Valley of Ten Thousand Smokes before volcanologists can understand what happened in 1912. On June 6 of that year the earth cracked open at the bottom of the west slope of Mount Katmai. A mass of 30 cubic kilometers of pumice, ash, and gas invaded the valley, filling it at some points to a height of over 600 feet. Entire forests were burned and amalgamated with this deposit. For days powerful explosions, localized in one fissure, ejected millions of tons of volcanic material. The heavi-est elements spread out to a radius of 600 miles; the finer dust was sucked up into the stratosphere, where it circulated for months above the northern hemisphere. At the same time the top of the cone of Katmai (7,900 feet) exploded and then abruptly collapsed, giving way to a caldera a mile and a half in diameter and 2,000 feet deep, whose altitude was only 6,500 feet. The collapse probably served to fill the vacuum left under the volcano when the reservoir of its magma emptied out into the valley.

1) At this point a new series of explosions dug out a depression at the west base. A dome of viscous lava, 800 feet in diameter and 195 feet high (the "Novarupta," or the new erupted), installed itself on the spot like a rough-surfaced pancake formed from the residual liquid, the lees still left in the reservoir emptied of its magma. This is probably the place where the flow of pumice and ash which was to cover the valley originated. The Novarupta stared out of its round, steel-gray eye at the scene of the crime.

2) Today the valley of desolation presents a very different scene. Wind, rain, and ice have eaten away the pumice and sculpted it into jagged cliffs, turrets, and lacy pinnacles which redden under the least ray of the sun.

Pages 48–49:

These two slender, proud needles, pointing to heaven, bear a strong resemblance to each other but are of very different origins. Ziwi (p. 48), in the Kapsiki Mountains of Cameroon, was born some fifteen million years ago. Its highly viscous lava rose straight up, like toothpaste from a tube, keeping the cylindrical shape of a volcanic chimney, to form this beautiful needle with highly colored vertical walls. Saint-Michel d'Aiguilhe, at Puy-en-Velay in France, has quite another story. Here, two million years ago, there was a cone made up of ash and scoriae, whose hidden chimney was stuffed with the hardened debris of previous explosions. Over the millennia wind, rain, and ice dismantled the volcano, stripping it of its coat of dust and exposing the 250-foot-high chimney. A flight of 268 stairs leads to the splendid 10th-century chapel at the summit.

2

Stone sentries of old

In Atakor, in the center of Hoggar (Algerian Sahara), 400 lava domes and needles have pierced the older basalt flow and stand like sentries molded out of millenary stone.

1) Here, at Essa, the overheated, liquefied lava overflowed its chimney and piled up into this silvery dome 2,400 feet in diameter and 1,000 feet high. In front of the monster, like petrified witnesses to its erection, rise the turrets of Imadouzene, ruins of a huge exploded dome.

2) This grandiose collection of frozen silhouettes, of muted organs, can be seen from the hermitage of Charles de Foucauld at Asekrem (8,950 feet). Volcanologists long speculated as to the length of time necessary for their formation. The eruption of Mount Pelée on the island of Martinique gave them a chance to observe the development of a lava needle. It grew, alternately rising and falling, at the rate of 75 feet a day until it attained a height of 1,000 feet. Had it not several times crumbled, this sugar loaf would have reached a height of 2,700 feet!

1

When Africa is torn apart . . .

For a distance of 4,000 miles, from the Red Sea to Mozambique, a major depression, a rift underlies East Africa, working to split it in two. Fifty million years from now Somaliland and the eastern regions of Ethiopia, Kenya, and Tanzania will be separated from continental Africa and form an island like Madagascar.

This great fault, shaken by earthquakes, is striped with gaping fractures, constellated by giant volcanoes and hidden springs. There are tawny soda lakes with a high salt content, because rainwater and rivers, in contact with lava, dissolve calcium and sodium, extracting from them a caustic liquid which accumulates in low places.

1) One of these salty lakes, Bogoria (Kenya), is surrounded by hot springs and geysers whose foaming is due to their sodium content. They prove that the area is fractured, that magma is below, near the surface, ready to escape when it finds a way.

2) This is what happened at the southern end of Lake Turkana (Kenya) tens of thousands of years ago. Magma broke out through fractures and rose up under the water. The abrupt contact between burning lava and shallow water gave birth to this magnificent, harmoniously shaped, low-lying cone. The natives compared its shape to that of an elephant's stomach and gave it the same name, Naboiyaton. Much later, small volcanoes surged up, this time on land, and their outpourings of glossy black lava flowed to the back edge of Naboiyaton.

Lake Turkana, formerly Rudolph, nearly 200 miles long, is the largest inland body of soda water in the world. Nicknamed "Jade Lake," it contains some twenty thousand crocodiles, which are at home in its salty, fish-abounding waters.

Did Columbus see Teide in eruption?

After Iceland and the Azores, the Canaries are the Atlantic islands with the greatest number of volcanoes. Over the last three centuries there have been eight eruptions: on Lanzarote from 1730 to 1736 and in 1824; on Tenerife in 1704, 1706, 1708, and

1909; in the southern part of La Palma in 1949 and 1971.

1) The Canaries were born of many successive eruptions. Sedimentary rocks are rare. All we see is some sand blown by the wind off the Sahara and a few calcareous beaches, where dark shingles, polished by the waves, look like the eggs of some prehistoric animal. (The photograph is of Lanzarote.)

2) El Piton, the recently established summit of Mount Teide (12,198 feet), like a giant octopus, stretches its lava tentacles over an older volcanic structure. The viscous flow slowly crawled on the slopes of the monster, depositing vitreous rocks in canals formed by lava streams. The crater, like a golden ciborium held up to heaven, exhales through its fumaroles, embroidering a lacy pattern of ice and sulphur.

Christopher Columbus speaks of a great fire raging on Tenerife in 1492. Was this perhaps the most recent eruption of Mount Teide? No geologist has been able to say. What is certain is that on the slopes there are cones and lava flows which date from only a few centuries ago. When will there be another eruption? Perhaps before very long . . .

Volcanic harmonies

1) The Valley of Kings, on the island of Bali (Indonesia), could be called a work of art because, generation after generation, man has shaped and sculpted the rich volcanic soil. Thousands of small rice fields rise, overlapping one another, on the steep mountain slopes, bordered by lacy lines of silver, ebony, and jade.

2) Another island is noteworthy for the same reason: Lanzarote, in the Canaries. Here too, with patient ingenuity, man has made himself an accomplice of the volcano. The island is parched and seems totally unsuited to agriculture. But man has accomplished a miracle. Although rain is rare, there is abundant nocturnal dew. And where the ground is covered with lapilli and volcanic ash, this dew does not evaporate under the morning sun. The thousands of tons of porous lava cast up by volcanic eruptions absorb the moisture and transmit it, by capillary action, to the underlying soil.

3) On Lanzarote there are high winds the year round. In order to shelter fig trees and grapevines men have dug deep hollows—like miniature craters—in the ash and bordered them with walls of lava, outlining what seems like an infinite number of circles and decking the black soil with wreaths of brown basalt.

Clouds of stone

"We are awaiting death at any moment.
A mountain has burst near here. We are covered
with ash, in some places ten feet and six feet deep.
All this began on June sixth. Night and day we light
lanterns. We cannot see daylight. We have no water,
the rivers are just ashes mixed with water.
Here are darkness and hell, thunder and noise.
I do not know whether it is day or night.
The earth is trembling, it lightens every minute.
It is terrible. We are praying."
Ivan Orloff, an Alaskan Eskimo fisherman
wrote thus to his wife when he was living through
the most violent eruption of the 20th century, that of Katmai
in 1912, which formed the Valley of Ten Thousand Smokes.

Page 59:

In Alaska, on March 30, 1977, a rising mass of magma met a boiling sheet of water, which was abruptly changed into an enormous column of steam, exploding violently, pulverizing rocks, spewing an enormous cloud of ash and instantly cutting out two craters in the old base of the region: the Ukinreks.

Continents adrift

The earth's surface is a gigantic puzzle made up of a dozen rigid plates separated by mid-ocean ridges, which clash and overlap under the volcanic arcs at the oceans' edges. It is at the boundary lines of these plates, which float over the sticky mass of underlying magma, that mountains are thrown up, earthquakes take place, and volcanoes erupt.

The best-known ridge is that of a range of undersea mountains running from north to south in the mid-Atlantic, rounding Africa, traveling up the Indian Ocean and entering the Gulf of Aden. It emerges at very few points, such as Iceland and Djibouti.

1) The rift of Thingvellir (Iceland) is a segment of this ridge, emerging from the sea, a boundary between the American and Eurasian plates. Dozens of scar-like fissures streak it, carving out basalt flows and pushing apart, by about an inch a year, the west and east (American and European) sides of the valley.

2) At the bottom of the Gulf of Tadjoura (Djibouti) the ridge, like that of an enormous whale, rises from the ocean and digs into Afar, where colossal forces pry Africa and Arabia apart. Like a furrow traced by a giant plow this fracture overturns ancient accumulations of basalt, creating chaotic ridges of cyclopean blocks. On November 7, 1978, the fractures were abruptly opened, dilating the area by about six feet. Magma burst forth from one of these fractures, creating a small volcano. A splendid illustration of the mechanism which regulates the drift of continents!

2

1

The earth cracks

1) Before its 1977 eruption the crater of Nyiragongo (Zaire) contained a lake of molten lava. Three overlapping platforms floated on the surface, rising and falling with the shifting level of the lake. In the course of this large-scale realignment the uppermost platform, 3,900 feet in diameter and 500 feet below the crater's rim, was cracked by deep crevices (the human figures at the left give an idea of their size). Under the impulsion of a powerful tide the lake regularly overflowed. Within a few seconds waves of red-hot lava unrolled over the top platform, seeping into its every fissure, enveloping and drowning everything, including the apparatus of visiting volcanologists, in a fine, vitreous film of meringue-like texture until it ran up against the vertical walls of the infernal cauldron. We explored the interior of Nyiragongo in 1973, between two such overflows. Since the catastrophic eruption of 1977 the crater has become a dizzying hole 2,000 feet deep, deprived of both lava lake and platforms (see also pp. 110-114).

2) Almost all volcanic eruptions begin with the opening of a fissure through which magma under pressure makes its escape. On April 5, 1977, the Piton de la Fournaise (Réunion) trembled. The stair-like fracture then opened still has intermittent flames and exhales a bluish gas, the last repercussion of the volcano's anger.

Pages 64-65:
Along the ridge segments we have described above, eruptions flow; along the island arcs they are explosive. The viscous lava, rich in gases, provokes violent explosions which eject great clouds of gas, cinders, and blocks such as the one which rose 5 miles into the air on the side of Mount Westdahl (island of Unimak, among the Aleutians of Alaska) when a crater nearly a mile in diameter was born in the middle of a glacier on February 4, 1978.

2

When a volcano attacks airplanes . . .

1) In 1976 Mount Augustine (Alaska) entered a phase of particularly violent activity. Mud flows and glowing clouds ravaged its snowy slopes, carrying away a geophysical observatory and burying its instruments. But this was not all. Spirals of volcanic ash and corrosive gases frosted the glass and abraded the paint of three Japanese commercial planes flying at an altitude of 33,000 feet.

When explosive eruptions of this kind are so powerful, the ash may be sucked into the upper atmosphere and linger there for weeks, months, even years. This was the case with the 18 cubic kilometers of volcanic dust ejected by Krakatau (Indonesia) between August 25 and 27, 1883. In the following months sunsets everywhere took on green and blue or red tints, because the light was refracted by volcanic particles. A more serious effect was a lowering of the temperature throughout the northern hemisphere. Curtains of opaque ash blocked the sun's rays, and the winters of 1883 and 1884 were especially severe. Similarly, in 1912 and 1913, the average world temperature was lowered one degree Celsius by the eruption of Katmai (Alaska).

Such eruptions, were they even more powerful, could explain the glacial periods of the earth's history.

2) Just as we reached the cone of Mount Colima (Mexico), the volcano greeted us with a plume of smoke gilded by the setting sun.

1

2

4

5

6

Volcanoes: steam machines of which we see only the chimneys

Gases are the motors of volcanic activity, just as they are of the bubbles in a champagne bottle. They are dissolved in magma, and their release and pressure impel molten rock toward the surface and precipitate an eruption.

Volcanic gases contain 60–90 percent of steam and lesser quantities of carbonic gas, sulphurous gases, carbon monoxide, hydrogen, nitrogen, hydrochloric and hydrofluoric acids. The amounts of these components vary with the temperature, pressure, and chemical composition of the magma.

1) Thanks to this device, an automatic chromatograph, the chemists of the "Vulcan" team analyzed gases inside the crater of Stromboli, a permanently active volcano in the Aeolian Islands (Sicily).

2) The Bocca Nuova, which made its appearance on one side of the central crater of Mount Etna (Sicily) in 1968, for over a year emitted spurts of gas at a speed of 350 miles an hour and a temperature of 1000° C.

3) On the small island of Paluweh (Indonesia), where there is no river or spring of any kind, fumaroles, made up of 99 percent steam, fizz out of the dry soil. The natives employ an ingenious system utilizing a vertical stalk of bamboo to catch the steam, and another one, in a diagonal position, to condense and convey it. In this way

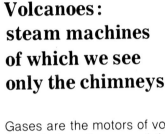

they obtain 100 gallons of pure, fresh water a day.

4) On Papandajan (Indonesia), when sulphurous gases make contact with the humid air they solidify and crystallize into clusters of sulphur which carpet the vents.

5) On Kawah Idjen (Indonesia) the activity of the fumaroles is so intense that every day it produces four tons of sulphur, which the Javanese are adept at extracting. The origin of sulphur remains a mystery. Volcanologists think that it comes from the core of the earth, some 1,800 miles deep down.

6) During its period of activity in July 1976, the volcano of Batur, on the island of Bali (Indonesia) alternated explosions with emissions of gas, as if the outlet were the safety valve of an enormous subterranean steam machine.

Page 68:
When Eldfell (Iceland) erupted in 1973 the hot flow pouring into the sea vaporized the icy ocean water into great white arabesques and transformed the port of Heimaey into a weird, unreal landscape enveloped in a warm fog. In the background a small volcano rumbled and panted, spitting its plume of ash and gas 4 miles up into the air.

Page 69:
The rain which fell upon the hot lava flow from the Piton de la Fournaise (Réunion) evaporates into a golden cloud in the eastern sky. A minute human figure in the background gives some idea of the size of this giant volcanic sauna.

Volcanic gases as sources of life

Volcanoes are the only openings that allow the earth to free itself of the gases dissolved in the deep-lying magma. Indeed, every year volcanoes spit out 100 million tons of sulphurous gases. In 1917 the Valley of the Ten Thousand Smokes (Alaska) alone emitted 125 million tons of hydrochloric acid and 200,000 tons of hydrofluoric acid. Laki (Iceland) ejected 20 million tons of carbonic

gas in the eight months of its activity. As for Vesuvius (Italy), during four days of eruption in 1929, it expelled a million tons of steam. These figures may seem astonishing, but laboratory experiments have shown that a single cubic kilometer of granite liberates 7 billion cubic meters of steam. And subterranean reserves of magma come to hundreds of thousands of cubic kilometers.

1) This pure white cloud escaping from the crater of Augustine (Alaska) bears witness to the quantity of steam involved in volcanoes. It is not surprising that much of the atmosphere

and all of the water on the earth's surface—lakes, rivers, and oceans—should have come originally, during the more than four billion years of our planet's existence, from fumaroles and other volcanic steam vents. The possibility of life on our planet is due to volcanoes.

2) An astronaut on the moon? No, this is Maurice Krafft on the edge of the crater of Stromboli (Italy). He is wearing a helmet made of plexiglass, which offers protection from the rain of volcanic bombs, and an oxygen mask, which allows him to breathe amid the toxic air of the volcano.

Blazing fireworks

"Here we have a foggy, smoky land,
More stinking than carrion, surrounded
by dark clouds and mists . . .
Sparks spring up from the abyss;
roaring wind projects the fire. No thunder
makes such a noise. Flames and burning stones fly so high
that they hide the light of day . . . Hell throws up to the sky
fire and flames, burning beams and scrap iron, pitch and sulphur;
then everything falls back down into the abyss."
This is an account of an Icelandic eruption
experienced in the 6th century by the monk Saint Brendan.

Page 75:
Spellbound, a volcanologist stands before the magic spectacle of lava fountains on the Piton de la Fournaise (Réunion).

1

Winter glow

To the general public volcanoes are giant furnaces, burning the year round. Actually, these devil's cauldrons are more like iceboxes than stoves. They are apt to reach an altitude of 6,500 to 10,000 feet, and to have the low temperatures, cloudiness, snow, rain, and wind typical of a mountain climate.

1) Pavlof (Alaska) is the most active volcano in North America, with twenty-six eruptions between 1700 and 1976 (year of its last eruption) repeatedly covering its snowy slopes with black ash. In 1973, while vertical jets of lava spurted from the summit, heavy glowing clouds rolled down the sides. The clear-cut line separating the snow from the ash shows that the latter was rigorously channeled. This separation allowed the celebrated volcanologist F. Perret to make his observations at a distance of less than 100 feet from the glowing avalanches which rained down from Mount Pelée (Martinique) in 1929–1930. Still, it took considerable courage to venture so close to the murderous fall of glowing ash.

2) Etna (Sicily), active for over a hundred thousand years, is a stratovolcano whose summit is 10,800 feet above sea level. The almost permanent explosive and effusive activity of the summit alternates with lateral eruptions on its slopes. One of these, which lasted from January 30 to March 29, 1974, built up two cones 980 feet high, the Monti di Fiori, among the pine forests of the western slope, at an altitude of 5,500 feet. There was some nervousness among the inhabitants of Bronte, a town lying just below the site of the eruptions.

Parabolas at play

Some nine thousand miles separate
these two scenes. At the left, Stromboli (Aeolian Islands, Italy) at sunset;
at the right, Batur (Bali, Indonesia) by
night. The long time exposure of the
camera has caught the perfect para-
bolic trajectories of volcanic bombs.
In order to find out how closely he
can, with safety, approach an eruption, a volcanologist observes these
trajectories and may even calculate
their end point and manage to avoid
it. If, when he is near the outlet, there
is a dense fall of bombs, then he must
run toward the explosion. He will be
safer under the curve of the trajectories than at their point of landing.

Silver ants

1) We prefer to avoid this dangerous game by outfitting ourselves with antishock fiberglass helmets resting on the shoulders and leaving the head and neck free but protected (Stromboli, Italy).

2) In this outfit the body cushions the impact of falling blocks and withstands the shock of a volcanic bomb weighing several pounds, at a temperature of 1000° C and falling from a height of 160 feet.

1

2

2

Stromboli: lighthouse of the ancient Mediterranean peoples

North of Sicily there is an island that rises to 3,000 feet above the sea and plunges to 6,500 feet below it. Stromboli (also known as Strongyle, the "spinning top" of the ancient world) is the only European volcano in a state of perpetual activity, producing an explosion every few minutes. For 2,000 years its flashes have guided navigators on the Mediterranean. If any volcano is worth visiting, Stromboli is it. Its summit, Cima, is 650 feet above the erupting crater, and from this vantage point the visitor can safely admire the monster's convulsions and the fireworks it produces so abundantly.

1) Up there lives a dragon. Feverish, toxic breath pours out of his enormous, gaping mouth, and his throat is filled with burning red lava.

2) The dragon gurgles and whistles until, suddenly, in a sharp spasm, his gaseous breath explodes and bursts into flame. He spews fire in an incandescent shower, then, exhausted, hiccoughs, grumbles, noisily catches his breath, falls back for a few seconds and begins all over. (Only two seconds elapsed between these two photographs.)

1) Men are emptying this house, only 330 yards away from Eldfell. A few hours later it was buried under 16 feet of ash.

2) In April the explosive force diminished, permitting the volcanologists of the Vulcan Team to approach within twenty feet of the crater. At this moment the magma, at a temperature of 1200°C, was in contact with the sea, creating an incandescent spray like that of a rocket, in which lava was transformed into bulging balls.

The saga of Eldfell

On January 23, 1973, at 1:55 a.m., began one of Iceland's most destructive eruptions. A fissure 5,200 feet long and 10 feet wide tore open the island of Heimaey at a distance of only 500 feet from a town of 5,000 inhabitants: Vestmannaeyjar ("the archipelago of the men of the West"). Fifty fountains of lava shot up along the fissure, making a 300-foot-high curtain of fire. Five thousand years had passed since there had been a similar episode of Earth's travail, the eruption of Helgafell, the island's other volcano. Now everything moved very fast. Ten minutes after the birth of the new monster—subsequently named Eldfell ("Fire Mountain")—the police sounded the alarm. Awakened by sirens, the inhabitants were amazed to see the great volcanic fire raging and roaring so short a distance away. At the capital, Reykjavík, 65 miles distant, Civil Defense experts feverishly discussed what to do and finally decided that Heimaey should be evacuated. Over a period of only a few hours in the middle of the night, in a courageous and disciplined way, the 5,000 inhabitants left the island. The aged and infirm were picked up by helicopters while the others made the four-hour voyage by boat to the south shore of Iceland. There all the buses of Reykjavík, requisitioned for the purpose, came to take the evacuees to the capital. Hotels and schools were put at their disposal, but, thanks to an extraordinary spirit of comradeship, every single one of the refugees was offered hospitality by a private household that same afternoon.

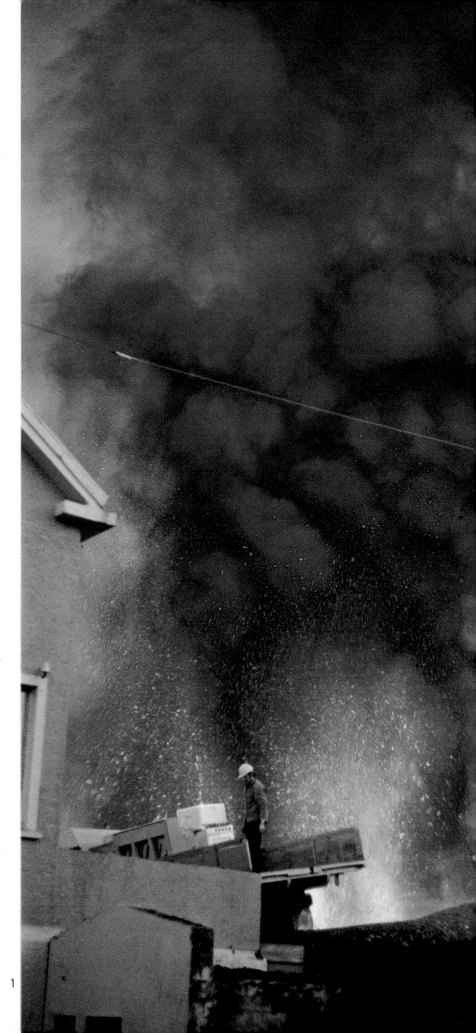

1

2

On January 24, volunteers returned to the island to empty the houses most threatened by Eldfell. The active section of the fissure was only 1,000 feet long; but three wide, rhythmically panting openings spewed 800-foot-high fountains of lava whose rise and fall were punctuated by explosions powerful enough to shatter glass and doors. On the evening of January 25 there was a major catastrophe. A rising wind drove the falling ash toward the town, which was soon buried, like a northern Pompeii, under hundreds of thousands of cubic meters of blocks and particles of lava. By the third day the houses nearest the volcano had disappeared under 30 feet of black mineral snow. In the center of the town the ash stood at 3 feet. Stretching out from this central point to a distance of over a mile from the eruption, houses were struck by volcanic bombs as much as 50 pounds in weight, which crashed through windows and rooftops and set fire to woodwork, furniture, curtains and carpets. Carrying on this unequal struggle around the clock, the firefighters rescued 800 automobiles, 2,500 tons of frozen and salted fish, and the contents of most of the houses. Fourteen thousand plates of corrugated iron were nailed to windows facing the volcano, and ash was swept from many rooftops before it could accumulate sufficiently to cave them in.

This was only the beginning of the extraordinary 157-day saga of Eldfell, in which brave, stubborn men stood up against the unleashed power of a volcano in order to save the island where they had been born (see pp. 116–119).

1) During the night of January 25–26, 1973, the lava fountains of Eldfell, gushing up to 650 feet high, ejected a half million cubic meters of incandescent ash and blocks of basalt.

2) This same night volcanic bombs set fire to fourteen houses.

Arabesques of fire

After long hours of walking through the chaos of lava blocks, reeling from fatigue, with our hands torn by rough, sharp fragments of volcanic glass, our faces lashed by an icy wind, we come at last to the crater and at once forget all our hardships before one of the most dazzling of all natural spectacles. Half suffocated by the volcano's alternately hoarse and shrill burning breath, we stare at the purple and gold spray rising up into the night. Nature's fireworks shoot tirelessly upward as if to reach the stars, pause for a moment and then fall back in splashes which roll down the mountainside like trails of blood.

Photography catches these spectacular outbursts in the symmetry of their incandescent curves, which stand out for a brief minute and then fade away into the night (Piton de la Fournaise, Réunion).

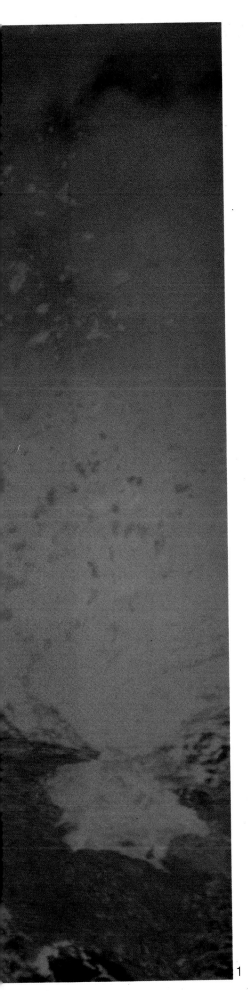

Descent into hell

Numerous·are the craters which we have explored and sounded, numerous our descents into the circles of Dante's hell, into the eyes of Vulcan staring up at the stars, into the places where the planet palpitates.

1) We have unforgettable memories of our stay in the crater of Nyiragongo (Zaire). Before its terrifying eruption of 1977 it provided a porthole opening to the entrails of our planet, a sight of incomparable power and beauty (see pp. 110–111). In 1973 we pitched our tents on the great platform bordering the lava lake (see pp. 62–63). Before going to bed every night we made a tour of our circular prison, whose 500-foot-high walls reflected the raging flames of the lake 30 feet below. The immense surface of molten rock, stirred by abrupt, spasmodic movements, burst into fantastic blazing showers as it struck the surrounding walls. At times the level of the lake was suddenly lowered by as much as 30 feet, as if the depths were sucking it in; then heavy waves of burning lava raised it to its former height. We had moments of fear, for during the preceding weeks the lava had several times overflowed our platform with a foam at 1200 °C. Molten rock would have risen to our knees and inflicted an atrocious death upon us. No chance of escape, but such are the risks of the job! In spite of the danger, we human ants never tired of the fantastic, constantly shifting, and diversely embellished spectacle. It was hard to tear ourselves away from the edge of the abyss and go back to our tents when clouds from above floated down into the crater, enveloping us in a purplish fog and hiding the restless movement in the uncovered pool of lava. Lying on the quivering ground, our faces burned by the feverish breath of Nyiragongo, impregnated with sulphur and deafened by the monster's rumbling and whistling, we were haunted by images of the incandescent storm.

2) Katia Krafft at the edge of an active crater of the Piton de la Fournaise (Réunion) in 1975.

The approach
to La Fournaise

Lava fountains at a temperature of 1200°C spurt from the crater which formed on November 4, 1975, on the Piton de la Fournaise (Réunion). In order to get within 10 feet of the edge and pick up samples of basalt, a geologist of the Vulcan group is wearing "Spirotechnique" overalls made of asbestos gauze with an aluminum coating which reflects 80 percent of infrared rays. Eyes are protected by strips of glass, alternating with gold leaf. The boots have thick soles which soften and stretch when treading hot ground, thereby making the feet sensitive to the presence of undetected lava from subterranean outlets. Insulating asbestos boots would not serve the purpose.

Earth's blood . . .

Blood of the planet Earth gushes out of a scratch in the crust (Piton de la Fournaise, Réunion). Like so many loose-jointed, purple-clad puppets, or scarlet many-footed animals, the lava fragments rise up, pause, fall back and re-emerge in the mad dance of the grumbling, whistling, sizzling volcano. Sometimes the monster's violent breath throws them up so high that they stretch, fall apart, burst, collide, join up again and then crumple at the edge of the yawning gap in the shape of frayed crimson bundles which fizzle and are then extinguished.

Destructive fever

"Fiery masses advance;
shapeless rock formations roll, in disorderly array, before them;
clouds of black sand take noisy flight . . .
Liquid elements start to boil harder and harder
and finally spill over into a sluggish river
which wends its way down the hillside . . .
Nothing can halt the fiery flow;
no dike can restrain it . . .
Finally the river cools off and slows down,
then hardens and gradually the fiery matter solidifies;
that which seemed to be a harvest of flames
takes on a new appearance . . ."
This is how Empedocles, the Greek philosopher
of the 5th century B.C., described the flow of lava
from Mount Etna, to which he retired toward the end of his life.

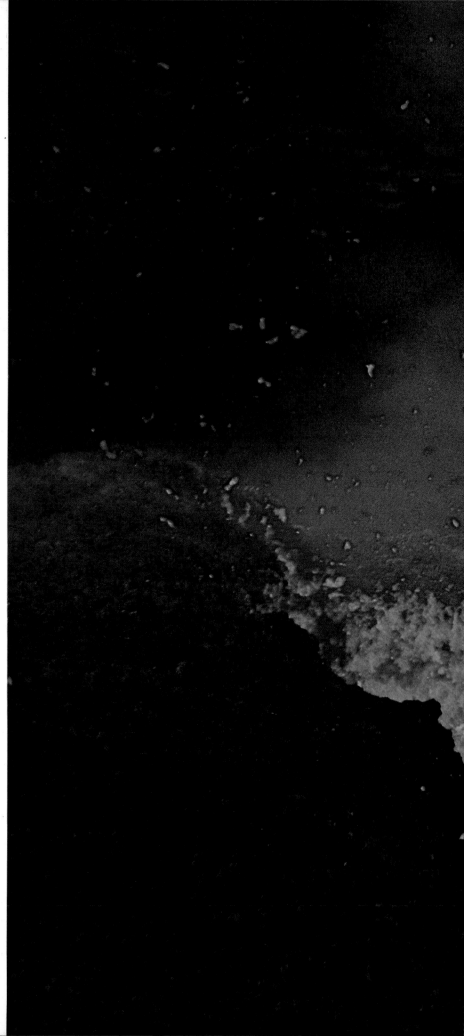

Page 97:
Near the summit of the Piton de la Fournaise (Réunion) the surface and edges of a lava flow, as they cool off and coagulate, sometimes form a tunnel in which molten rock continues to move. This lava-roofed cave is 12 feet high, 12 feet wide, and perhaps 100 feet long.

Earth: a giant nuclear power station

What about fire at the heart of our planet? There can be no such fire, because combustion requires free oxygen, and it does not exist in this form in the depths of the earth. What is there, then? There is fusion, like that of a great steel mill. Rocks are melted by heat which is the product of their own radioactivity. Whether they are sedimentary, metamorphic, or volcanic, they contain small quantities of radioactive elements, such as uranium, thorium, and potassium 40, which, over millions of years, are spontaneously transformed into other, more stable elements. These transformations produce energy and hence heat; for this reason the earth is hot. Indeed, it is a gigantic nuclear center which has been in business for 4.7 billion years and which has sufficient radioactive elements to stay in business for billions of years to come. The process of nuclear disintegration is very slow. It takes a cubic centimeter of granite 500 million years to free, by radioactivity, the heat necessary to warm up a cup of coffee.

This enormous lava bubble exploding from a crater at the summit of the Piton de la Fournaise (Réunion) is proof of the heat-producing capacity of our planet.

1

Melted gold rose
out of the earth . . .

In the 16th century some scientists believed that the lava of certain volcanoes was melted gold. Two Spanish monks—Brothers Blas del Castillo and Juan de Gandavo—swindled their countrymen by founding a company for the purpose of exploiting the gold that flowed from the volcano of Mount Masaya in Nicaragua. Needless to say, the only profit was that pocketed by the two swindlers.

1 and 2) During the eruptions of the Piton de la Fournaise (Réunion) the stream of lava is abundant and liquid, attaining a speed of 35 miles an hour. The rapidity of such a flow depends on the temperature of the molten rock, its chemical composition, its gas content, and the steepness of the slope. There is lava which advances at a speed of only a few inches a day, and that which reaches a velocity of 50 miles an hour. With respect to volume, it varies considerably from one eruption to another. The largest lava flow in history was that of Laki in Iceland, in the year 1783. In June of that year a 15-mile fracture opened up and was soon crowned by 115 craters. In the course of eight months, 12 cubic kilometers of lava covered a surface of 218 square miles. The output of molten rock was at the rate of 5,000 cubic meters per second, which is twice the amount of water expelled from the mouth of the Rhine River. The longest single stream measured 35 miles.

"From these overflowing abysses arises Vulcan's fire."
(Empedocles)

Dozens of eruptions have taken place at the summit of the Piton de la Fournaise (Réunion) without in the least disquieting the local population. Most of them have occurred inside l'Enclos, the 6,500-foot-high, uninhabited caldera of the volcano. On March 24, 1977, a fissure opened up at an altitude of 6,500 feet, and out of it lava spurted and flowed. A few hours later calm was restored. On April 5 there was an identical second eruption, which lasted for only two days. La Fournaise is subject to such minor crises; they are commonplace occurrences. But on April 8 the lava broke through to the exterior of l'Enclos, amid the mountainside vegetation, at an altitude of 3,600 feet, and rushed down toward the little village of Bois-Blanc, which was hastily evacuated. Fortunately, it came to a halt before reaching the first houses. The following day another fissure opened at an altitude of 2,600 feet and lava was precipitated at 25 miles per hour into another village, Piton Saint-Rose, crashing through the tropical forest and the fields of sugarcane, cutting a road and swallowing up twelve evacuated houses before pouring into the sea where, on a 1,600-foot front, fire and water clashed. Other, even more rapid surges followed, devouring twenty more houses, surrounding the police station, and burning up the wooden door to a church in whose nave they finally came to rest. Only on April 16, after it had vomited over 4 million cubic meters of basalt, was the eruption definitely over.

Aa and pahoehoe

When Mount Etna erupted in 1974 the lava burned thousands of trees as it wound slowly through the pine forests. In the process of hardening it crumbled and piled up in blocks of rough-surfaced slag. It is particularly hard to cross a slaggy area on foot. The rocks, piled up in unstable equilibrium, roll over; the jagged scoriae cut through the soles of shoes and scratch the hands. The natives of Hawaii, where such formations are very common, call them ''aa,'' mimicking the sound aroused by the pain of treading on them barefoot. There is, on the other hand, hardened lava which has a smooth surface, interrupted only by swirls and rope-like wrinkles. This the Hawaiians call ''pahoehoe,'' which means satiny. Today geologists the world over use these words to designate the two different kinds of hardened lava.

In 1920 the volcanologist R. H. Finch had a curious adventure while he was studying the formations of ''aa'' lava on the slopes of Kilauea in Hawaii. One day at lunchtime he sat down among a pile of still warm blocks of lava. Looking around as he ate, he exclaimed to himself: ''The landscape is moving!'' Then he realized that the tepid ''aa'' lava was still on the move. Amused by the unusual character of this type of navigation, he calmly ate his lunch.

The incredible voyage of Popkov and Ivanov

In 1938, during the eruption of a parasitic cone on the flank of Kliutchevskaia on the Kamchatka peninsula (Siberia), two intrepid Russian volcanologists, intent upon securing accurate readings of temperature, undertook to mount a block of solidified lava which was floating, at a speed of 100 feet a minute, on the surface of a river of molten rock at 870°C. V. F. Popkov and I. Ivanov navigated on

this raft for more than an hour for a distance of over a mile, measuring the temperature and taking samples of gas. The temperature of their improvised craft was 300°C so that, even with their asbestos boots, they had to stand on first one foot and then the other.

1) The Piton de la Fournaise (Réunion) is a favorite site for study by volcanologists, because its eruptions are both frequent and accessible. Thanks to a special thermometer, we were able to take a temperature of 1134°C in this flow, which, after pursuing a long underground course, had

surfaced and was winding its incandescent way aboveground toward the sea.

2) Maurice Krafft, protected by a fire-resistant suit, wrested this fragment of burning lava from the heart of the flow. Chemical analysis of basalt in this state (expressed in oxides) shows 44 percent silicon, 21 percent magnesium, 15 percent iron, 8 percent aluminum, 7 percent calcium, 2 percent sodium, 2 percent titanium, and traces of potassium, phosphorus and manganese.

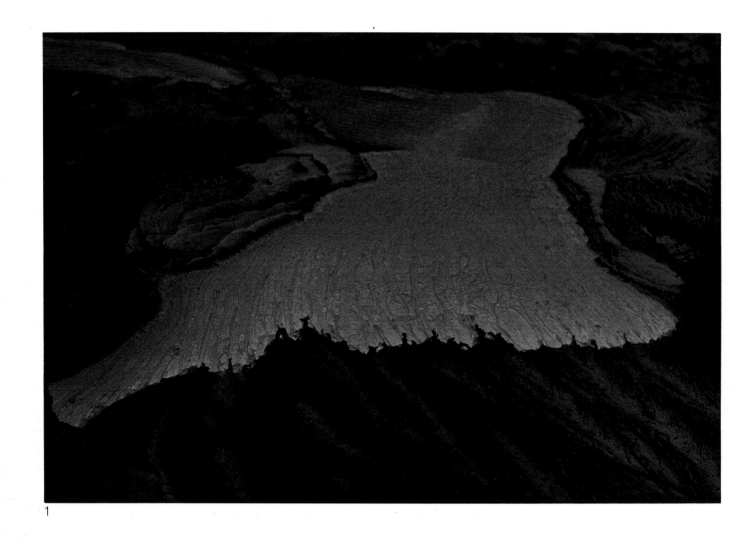

1

Vulcan's lanterns

1) Surging up from a bowl with a jagged rim, this lava stretches its vermilion flow into a sinuous stream which, advancing curve by curve, throws itself, hissing, into the sea. The flaming throat of the mythical giant is silenced in the primitive waters.

2) Sometimes the fiery serpent loses its way, falters, writhes, folds, and swirls as it advances over the body of already solidified lava. Slowly the purple and gold excrescences halt and are extinguished, crackling like bread fresh from the oven.

In both cases the lava is of the pahoehoe type, ejected by the Piton de la Fournaise (Réunion) in March 1976.

1

A mass of purple and gold turned into a silver shroud

1) Between 1928 and 1977 Nyira-gongo (Zaire), situated on the west fork of the Great Rift of East Africa, offered volcanologists the most grandiose spectacle Earth can pro-duce: a lake of lava in a state of con-tinuous melting. In 1973 the lake was shaped like a crescent, 980 feet long and 330 feet wide, churned by a heavy groundswell. Gases exploded in golden balls on the incandescent surface, ran close to the rim, and pro-duced jets of dazzling yellow.

2) When the agitation of the lake subsided, the surface was covered by a partially cooled, gray, wrinkled skin, like that of an elephant. This split up into segments bordered by jagged, glowing lines. Then, all of a sudden, the molten mass underneath this skin was violently churned up and caused the segments to circulate. Here we had a small-scale and accelerated re-production of the continental drift of the earth over millions of years. In the middle of the lake the segments fell apart, offering passageway to newly risen fluid lava. At the edges they bumped, overlapped, plunged and were gradually swallowed up, in an admirable dance, by the underlying magma.

Unfortunately, this natural wonder violently disappeared in 1977, sowing death and desolation around the vol-cano. At the end of December 1976 the entire region was shaken by several earthquakes, and the lava lake reached a record high level of

0,700 feet of altitude, threatening he town of Goma, 5,500 feet below. The pressure exerted by the column f lava was enormous. On January 0, 1977, at quarter past ten in the morning, the volcano abruptly gave vay and five large north-south fis-ures opened up on its sides. In less han an hour the whole crater was mptied, like a collapsing dam, and 3 million cubic meters of molten ock spilled down the slopes of the olcano at a speed of 25 miles an our, enveloping woods, valleys, elds and villages, and leaving the in-habitants little time in which to flee. The lava was so hot and liquid that it traveled uphill, pushed against every obstacle in its way, surrounded and enveloped trees and swallowed up men, houses, and even automobiles. The final reckoning calculated 400 houses destroyed, 3,000 acres of fields and woodland submerged by lava. As for the human victims, figures vary from 60 to 2,000.

Page 112:
The great lava flow of Nyiragongo (Zaire) covered some six miles of highway. Automobiles and trucks on the road during the eruption were overturned and burned by the tidal wave of molten rocks. Only much later were the shattered bodies of vehicles, such as the truck illustrated here, discovered.

Page 113:
Nothing is left of the shacks along the road except parts of their cellars, enveloped in silky lava. A sterile, si-lent, silvery desert, studded with car-bonized trees, occupies the space where, once upon a time, there were lively villages, green forests and fer-tile fields.

Parícutin: a volcano born in a field

On February 20, 1943, at four o'clock in the afternoon, Dionisio Pulido was working his field, a mile distant from the village of Parícutin (Mexico), when the earth suddenly opened up before him and a rumbling noise underneath his feet made him wonder whether he was going crazy. Trees wavered, the ground swelled, whistling steam came out of the crack, there was a strong smell of sulphur, then flames rose up and a pine tree caught fire. The terrified Dionisio ran to Parícutin to alert the inhabitants. When he returned to his field the next morning it was no longer there. A 30-foot-high cone of black ash, spitting gas and incandescent stones, oc-cupied the site. By noon, the new-born volcano, christened Parícutin, stood 150 feet high. A week later the height was 450 feet, and the rumbling sound could be heard 200 miles away. Later, dozens of incandescent streams rolled down its sides, cover-ing a wide surrounding area. In less than a year, fields, orchards, pine for-ests and human dwellings within a five-mile radius disappeared under either a thick coating of sterile ash or a blind stream of lava, leaving home-less the 6,000 inhabitants of the vil-lage and of the larger, nearby town of San Juan Parangaricutiro. For a period of more than nine years this "bad boy" of Mexico went on a rampage, ejecting 3,500 million tons of ash, bombs, and lava flows and eventually covering a 15-square-mile area with great blocks, to a thickness of 800 feet in places.

1) Today the tower of the cathedral of San Juan Parangaricutiro rises, like a lighthouse, from a wild sea of dark lava, marking the site of the buried town. In the background is the guilty one, the cone of Parícutin (1,345 feet).

2 and 3) The little Mexican volcano did not take any human lives. But the eruption of Mount Pelée (Martinique) on May 8, 1902, was one of the great catastrophes of the century. That day a glowing avalanche at a temperature of 600°C swept down the slopes of the volcano at a speed of 60 miles an hour, tumbling houses as if they were made of cardboard, sweeping away the cathedral, tearing up trees, and even sinking ships in the harbor. In a few minutes the volcano annihilated Saint-Pierre, the "Paris of the An-tilles," killing 28,000 inhabitants. Only two people—a prisoner in solitary confinement, and a shoemaker—es-caped alive.

Witnesses to the all-enveloping fire which followed upon the passage of the ash cloud are these two vases and the heap of nails, partially melted by the flames.

Seawater to
fight a volcano

When Eldfell, on the island of Heimaey, south of Iceland, erupted in
1973, men pitted their strength
against that of the devouring monster
in an epic David-versus-Goliath con-
test. When the volcanic activity first
showed itself they were satisfied with
dismantling and moving out their pos-
sessions in order not to lose them if
the town were to be threatened (see
pp. 84–87). But as they became
aware of the eruption's destructive

power they decided to sidetrack and
perhaps halt the enormous flow of
chaotic and viscous lava which was
laying waste to their homes and pushing on inexorably toward the harbor.
Heimaey is, in fact, the most important port of the Icelandic fishing
fleet.

During the early days the lava flow
from Eldfell steadily gained speed. On
February 12 all shipping left the port.
The exit had been reduced to a width
of a hundred feet and the temperature of the bay water had risen to
32°C. On March 6 it seemed as if the
battle were lost. The molten rock, in
an access of speed, was touching the

piers. Half skeptically the Icelanders
launched 1,250 tons of seawater per
hour from two fireboats against the
advancing front of basalt. After contact with the jet of cold water the flow
slowed down and solidified. But this
triumph was of short duration because a new jet of magma rose out of
the crater and made straight for the
town. Like a bulldozer, the molten
mass proceeded, street by street,
crushing, burning, and swallowing up
one house after another. Three
hundred buildings, the swimming
pool, and the power plant were wiped
off the map. Next, the lava front, nearly 1,000 feet wide, headed for the fish-

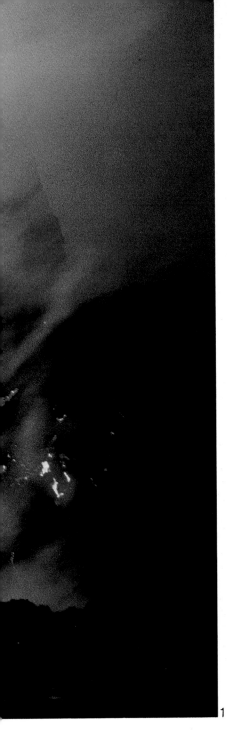

800°C, and at this temperature it no longer flowed. The arrested and solidifying lava formed a wall, a natural dike, which contained the flow behind it. As soon as the temperature permitted, the Icelanders moved the pipes farther upstream, to points where the heat was greater, solidifying, little by little, all the sources of molten rock. This operation, of two months' duration, was an unqualified success. Six million cubic meters of seawater blocked the motion of 4.5 million cubic meters of lava. The port of Heimaey was saved and, ironically

enough, it was protected against future eruptions. The area of the island was increased by one and a half square miles.

1) The lava flow from Eldfell advances by successive overflowings toward the ocean. Upon contact the seawater is transformed into clouds of steam.

2) Ramparts of scoriae are steamrollered and built up into a dam which stems the advancing flow of lava.

3) Men carry upstream the pipes which are to pour seawater on the lava.

2

3

1

freezing plant and destroyed two of its five buildings. From there, the flow moved on toward the harbor. If it were blocked, Heimaey would be done for. At this point the Icelanders braced themselves for a last combat. Forty-three powerful pumps were brought in by air freight from the United States and installed on the piers in the course of a single night. Two days later an 18-mile-long chain of pipes made it possible to direct 4,000 tons of seawater per hour, twenty-four hours a day, against the advancing wall of lava. Thanks to this jet of cold water, the temperature of the basalt was lowered from 1000 to

"You have lived, and you will live again . . ."

1) This sentence, engraved on the gate to the cemetery of Heimaey, buried under six feet of ash, could be the motto of the submerged city.

2) In the eastern part of the island dozens of houses disappeared under fifteen feet of volcanic dust. During 157 days of activity Eldfell threw up 20 million cubic meters of ash and 230 cubic meters of flowing lava. On June 28, 1973, activity ceased, and the townspeople returned. Houses were freed of their ashen shroud and repainted; cracks were filled and broken windows replaced. The tons of ash that had been swept up were used to enlarge the local airstrip and to build four hundred new houses to replace those totally destroyed.

3) As soon as the volcano stopped erupting, the people worked to stabilize the ash on the new cone, which swept down into the town with every gust of wind. They scattered grass seed from an airplane and stretched old fishnets over the slopes, but all to no avail. During the summers of 1974 and 1975 hundreds of student volunteers lent a hand. They removed the ash from around the town all the way to the mountain slopes and sowed grass seed by hand.

In spite of the generosity of other countries and the levy of a special tax in Iceland for relief to the homeless, Heimaey has had a difficult rebirth. But by dint of their stubborn courage the inhabitants have made a comeback. By 1975, 4,500 out of the 5,300

118

previous householders had returned.
Today the nightmare is forgotten, and
there are plans to use the residual
heat of the volcano for heating the
town. Eldfell transformed into a central
heating system, a destructive
force converted into benevolence! . . .

Benevolent matter

"Today calm reigns.
We acknowledge it with surprise in this abandoned landscape,
where thousands of volcanoes responded to one another
with their great subterranean organs
in the days when they spat fire.
Now we fly over a land struck dumb, decked with black glaciers.
Farther away, older volcanoes are dressed in golden grass.
In their hollows there grows an occasional tree,
like a flower in an old pot . . .
The last craters are filling up.
A grassy lawn harmonizes the curves of the volcanoes;
now they are all mildness.
Every fissure is sewn up by this tender linen.
Earth is smooth, slopes are gradual,
and we forget where they came from.
This lawn wipes out the dark sign from the slopes of the mountain."

(A. de Saint-Exupéry, *Wind, Sand and Stars*)

2

Earth's entrails

On the slopes of the Piton de la Fournaise (Réunion) we often walked over streams of lava whose surface had hardened within the hour. Below the thin skin on which we were treading, we glimpsed the scarlet incandescence of the molten rock. Often a surge of heat melted the soles of our shoes. At times a hole opened up and a molten subterranean current emerged into the air, then submerged again into a labyrinth of sub-lava tunnels.

1) In April 1977, lava spilled out over the slope of the Piton de la Fournaise at a speed of 50 miles an hour. Like a mountain stream the flow of liquified basalt side slipped on the curves and fell back into rolls of purplish fire, while its edges turned into slender stalactites.

2 and 3) In 1976, on the contrary, on the slopes of the same volcano, the flow of lava was slow; it folded and wrinkled into intricate ropes or swelled into sausages and tripe amid the sizzling sound of pie crust.

3

Page 121:
An aperture into Earth's entrails, a sub-lava tunnel on the slopes of the Piton de la Fournaise (Réunion).

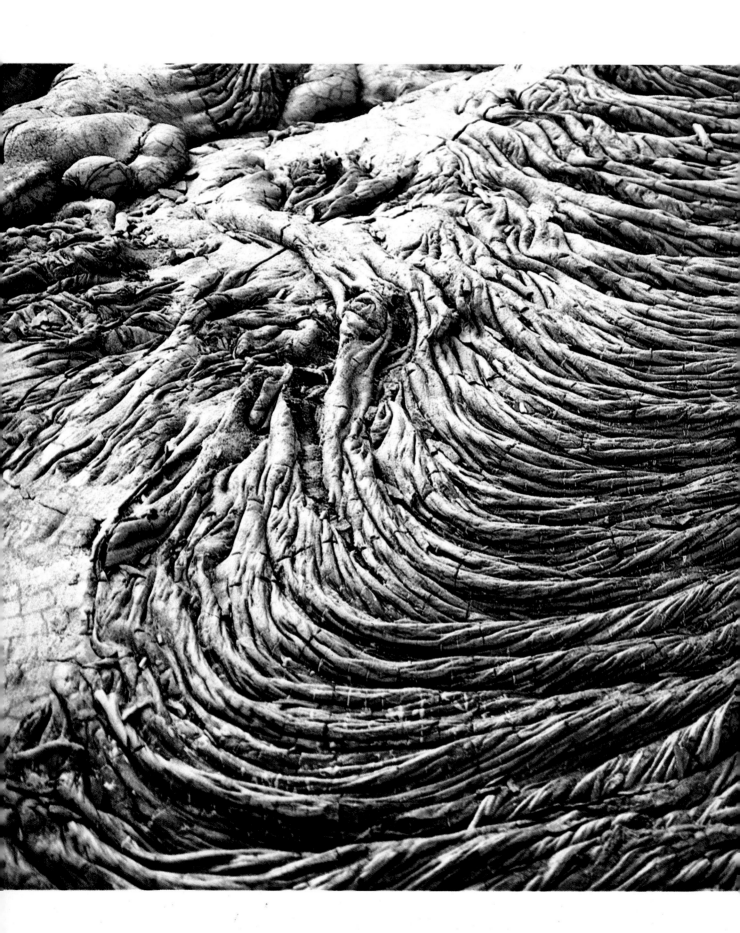

Bananas growing out of the lava flow

When a flow of very hot liquid basalt slows down it is soon covered with a skin whose temperature is lower than that of the liquid depths beneath it. The underlying lava, still in motion, pulls this crust along, misshaping, stretching, wrinkling, folding, and twisting it at the whim of the currents below. The underlying current of the flow is stronger at the center than at the sides, with the result that the folded skin at the surface is pulled downstream and falls into thousands of side-by-side coils.

1) This is what happened with the satiny coils, coated with a thin, silvery, vitreous substance which formed during the activity of the Piton de la Fournaise (Réunion) in 1976.

2) With the passage of the years the vitreous coating wears out, baring the basalt wrinkles, now overgrown with lichens and ferns whose tender green lights up the somber gray of this flow of lava from Mount Nya-muragira in Kivu (Zaire).

For weeks, months, and some-times years the bottom-layer lava stays warm, because it is a poor con-ductor of heat. A lava stream 300 feet thick takes three hundred years to cool completely. At Parícutin (Mexi-co), twenty-six years after the end of the volcano's activity, wood can be fired from contact with the lava on the upper slopes of the cone.

Farmers at the southern end of the island of La Palma (Canaries) noticed that banana trees grew faster when planted in warm soil. They flattened the uneven surface of a lava flow in 1971 from Mount Teneguia, covered it with a layer of soil and planted it with banana trees. The local people look forward to new eruptions, with the idea of augmenting their planta-tions. Their hopefulness is further justified by the fact that the last erup-tion did not damage their fields or vil-lages. The flow ran straight into the sea, enlarging the area of the island by several square miles.

Volcanic tears

1) On the Piton de la Fournaise (Réunion), when the basalt is especially liquid and the explosions especially strong, a spray of burning particles of rock, which cool upon contact with the air, descends upon the cone in showers of smooth, shiny "lava tears" only fractions of an inch in diameter.

2) On this same volcano, the impulsion of gases or the strength of the wind may turn the lava drops into silky black or reddish-brown threads several inches long, called "Pele's hair," in honor of the Hawaiian goddess of this name. This glass wool may be carried very far from the volcano, contaminating pastures and endangering the life of grazing animals if the needle-sharp glass perforates their intestines. In Hawaii, on the contrary, birds use "Pele's hair" to build their nests.

3) Very liquid flows may form such natural curiosities as these stalactites and stalagmites some six inches high on the walls of a sub-lava cave of Lanzarote (Canary Islands). When a flow passes through the lava tunnel, the combustion of gases at the surface reaches a temperature o

1400°C. This remelts the ceiling of the cave, forming twisted stalactites and stalagmites shaped like ears of corn.

4) If the lava ejected from the crater is thick and rich in volatile elements, its trajectory does not impress any shape upon it. But gases escaping from the molten mass swell the interior of the bomb into a spongy foam and mark its already hardened vitreous surface with cracks like those of an almost overcooked loaf of bread. This "bread loaf" bomb was ejected by the Augustine volcano (Alaska) in 1976.

Embracing bodies turned to stone

After the rumbling of the volcano, silence falls upon the petrified lava flow. The virgin matter which boiled up from the center of the earth crunches under the first footstep o man. *Above:* winds caress the en twined bodies, imprisoned in thei matrix of bronzed glass. *Right:* wave of bluish basalt swirl under the curve figure of a sleeping nymph (Piton d la Fournaise, Réunion).

1

When the great organs
of the monsters
fell silent

1) The *Roche Tuilière* ("Tile Rock"), at the heart of the Massif Central (France), is the remnant of an old volcanic chimney built up millions of years ago and stripped by erosion of its cone of ash. The prisms of gray-green phonolite are due to fissures which cut the lava into pentagonal or hexagonal columns when it cooled and contracted. (The process is the same as that by which caked mud around a pond breaks up into hexagons.) The people of Auvergne gave this formation its name because, for centuries, they used the rock to make roof tiles.

2) In the green oasis of Skaftafell (Iceland) these magnificent beehive draperies form the background of an icy waterfall which cascades down the side of the enormous Vatnajökull glacier.

1

The scratches of gigantic bear claws

1) Wind, rain, ice, and seawater patiently attack and erode congealed lava. And erosion, baring the heart of a volcano, pierces the mystery of its depths. In this case it reveals the symmetrical structure of a forest of connecting prisms on the island of Gomera (Canaries). Volcanologists attribute these shapes to the contrac-tion of lava. But in Wyoming (U.S.A.) the Kiowa Indians have a less rational but more poetic explanation of the slender colonnades of Devils Tower, which rise 850 feet above the surrounding land. Once upon a time, they say, seven little girls at play far from home were pursued by bears. Realizing that they could never get back to their village and find refuge there, they leaped onto a rocky crag and implored its aid. Immediately the rock rose straight upward until it touched the sky, where the little girls

were transformed into stars: the Pleiades. The bears tried to claw their way up the crag in their pursuit. But their efforts were in vain; only the scratches made by their claws, the organ pipes of Devils Tower, remain as a record of their endeavor.

2) When erosion takes an aggressive turn it dismantles the prisms. At Hljodaklettar the violent winds from Iceland have pierced them with a thousand cavities.

The devil's cauldron as a source of energy

In thermal zones the clay formed by the alteration of volcanic rock in its passage through fumaroles mingles with the water of the hot springs and turns into lugubrious gray mud. Gases with the stench of rotten eggs, due to their content of hydrogen sulphide, surge up in this satanic soup in the form of big bubbles which swell, gurgle, and finally burst into a viscous spray. In Iceland **(1 and 2)** and Indonesia **(3)** and in most other volcanic regions there are many such devil's cauldrons. But aside from their picturesque aspect, sometimes frightening, sometimes merely intriguing, these areas have an economic importance—based, in the past, on the hydrotherapy of spas and watering-places, and, today, on the new science of geothermics. The first large-scale experiments in this field were made at the turn of the century in Larderello (Italy). Holes were drilled to a depth of several hundred feet in order to catch the hot steam stored between a reservoir of magma and the protective, watertight layer en-

closing it. From 50 to 100 metric tons of steam per hour, at a temperature between 150 and 260° C and at a pressure between 5 and 40 atmospheres, spurted up from every hole and activated turbines that provided electricity for the railways of central Italy.

Thirteen countries—including the United States, New Zealand, Japan, Mexico, and Iceland—now exploit this means of producing electrical energy. In Iceland the main use is domestic. Almost all houses, 80 swimming pools, and 40 acres of greenhouses are heated by natural hot water. Even in France, in the Paris Basin, 16,000 apartments obtain their heating from 60° C water tapped at a depth of 4,900 feet. By 1990, five hundred thousand French homes should be able to enjoy the benefits of this system. With increasing awareness of the energy crisis and the dangers of nuclear power, the science of geothermics has suddenly acquired much more vital importance. Its future is assured, since billions of years will go by before our planet cools off . . .

A geyser
1,500 feet high

Geysers—that is, intermittent hot springs—are numerous in Iceland, the United States, and New Zealand. The most important of these, Waimangu, was in New Zealand. Between 1890 and 1904 it ejected 200,000 gallons of water to a height of 1,500 feet every few hours. At Geysir, in Iceland, we have the formerly active but now quiescent Great Geyser. (The Icelandic word is *gjòsa;* the term *geyser* originated here.)

2, 3 and p. 138) Fortunately, Great Geyser's neighbor, Strokkur, is carrying on the tradition. Every few minutes, accompanied by a hoarse noise, its surface swells into an enormous crystallized ball which bursts into a white spray consisting of thousands of tiny drops that rise to nearly 100 feet before they fall, ponderously, into the sky-blue basin of the panting monster.

1) Farther north, at Hveravellir ("Hot Valley"), small geysers gargle and then spit up sulphurous water, embroidering delicate sulphur wreaths around the smoke holes.

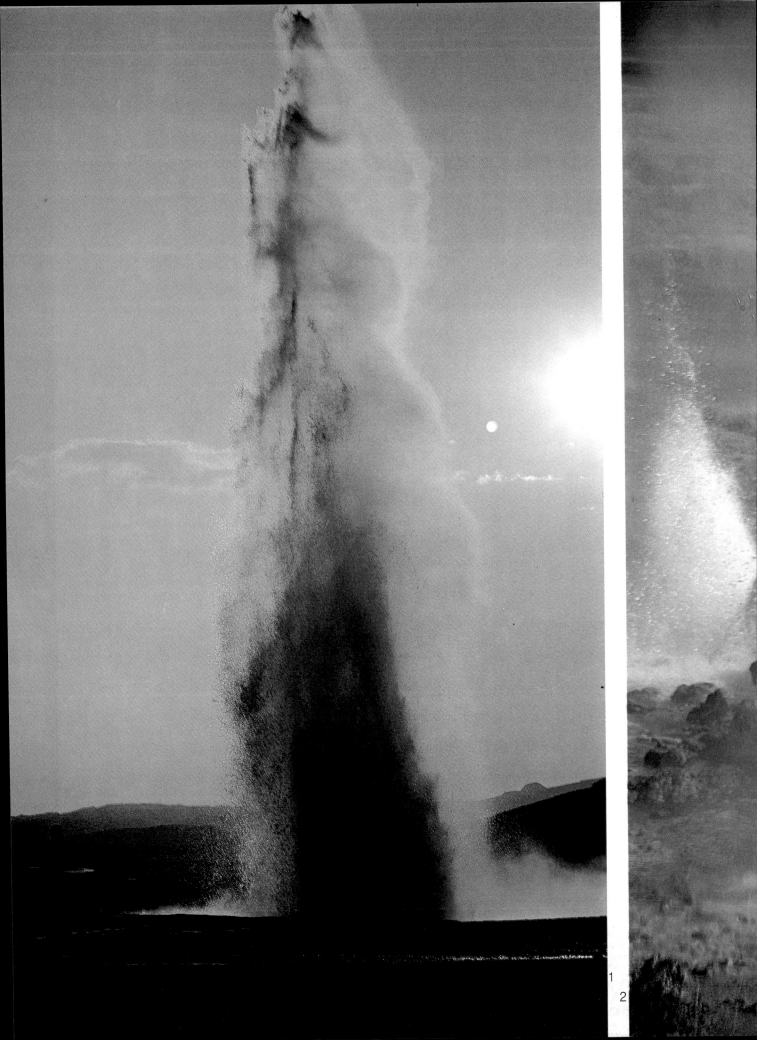

1
2

Soap: a trigger to activate geysers

The functioning of a geyser is a complex phenomenon. Water accumulates in a vertical duct, from 10 to 100 feet long, and gradually warms up through contact with an underground source of heat. At the bottom of the well, thanks to the pressure of the column of water, the liquid reaches a temperature of 103 to 104° C without boiling; it is superheated and hence unstable. The slightest change—for example, a rise of the liquid toward a zone of lesser pressure, or the presence of a gas bubble or of a solid particle—may cause the liquid to turn abruptly into steam, provoking an explosion which ejects both steam and water into the air. The water then falls back into the well, where it is reheated until—minutes, hours, or days later—the process is repeated.

In certain cases this phenomenon can be provoked artificially by the application of soap, whose foam breaks up connections between the molecules of water and thus vaporizes it. A Chinese laundryman made this discovery, involuntarily and to his own detriment, at Yellowstone National Park. Two days after he had opened up a laundry, which was to make use of the free water from hot springs, he was distressed to find that the springs were turning into increasingly more violent geysers, activated by the soapy water which he had discarded The next day an explosion scalded the poor man and wrecked his place of business. Since that time, there has been no laundry at Yellowstone.

1) The waters of Strokkur (Iceland), rich in silicon dioxide, precipitate lacy jets of white geyserite.

2) The geyser of Lake Bogoria (Kenya) is depositing rounded fragments of limestone (optical effects have sextupled the geyser's height).

A turquoise mounted in gold and ivory

This magnificent caldera crowning the summit of Mount Katmai (Alaska) resulted from a succession of colossal breakdowns caused by volcanic activity in the Valley of Ten Thousand Smokes in June 1912. The caldera, which is two and a half miles in diameter and has an average depth of 3,300 feet, contains rainwater, with remnants of sulphur, which give it its intense blue color and the aspect of a turquoise mounted in ivory and old gold. The lake grows in volume every year, so that by the year 2050 it should overflow.

The Spaniards of the Canary Islands and the Portuguese of the Azores were the first to apply the word "caldera" to volcanic depressions in the shape of a pot or cauldron. Today volcanologists give this name to craters with a diameter of over a mile. They often appear late in the history of a volcano, as the culmination of a long period of activity with its attendant emissions of lava flow, ash, pumice, and glowing avalanches. A mammoth explosion decapitates a volcanic cone, or else the roof of an underlying magma chamber, emptied by successive eruptions, collapses. The largest known calderas are La Garita (U.S.A.), with a diameter of 28 miles; Buldir (Alaska), 19 miles; Valles (U.S.A.) and Aso San (Japan), both 13 miles; Kawah Idjen (Indonesia) and Bolsena (Italy), both 11 miles; Aniakchak (Alaska), Santorin (Greece), and the Piton de la Fournaise (Réunion), all 5½ miles; Krakatau, Tengger and Batur (Indonesia), all 5 miles.

1

Satan's soup

Occasionally, with the passage of time, the bottom of a crater becomes carpeted with impermeable clay resulting from the decomposition of volcanic rock by fumaroles. Rainwater and rivulets accumulate and create crater lakes such as the celebrated Pavin in the Massif Central (France). If acid volcanic gases, charged with corrosive elements, continue to well up on the bottom, they change the sweet water of the lake into "Satan's soup."

1) Thus, Kawah Idjen, the "green crater" in the eastern part of Java (In-donesia) is occupied by a lake of vitriol, the only one of its kind, which contains a veritable fortune: 1.3 million tons of aluminum sulphate, 600,000 tons of hydrochloric acid, 550,000 tons of sulphuric acid, 200,000 tons of aluminum, 170,000 tons of iron sulphate, 140,000 tons of sulphate of magnesium, 120,000 tons of calcium sulphate, and 90,000 tons of potassium sulphate. But no one has dared to extract this treasure (36 million cubic meters of mineral liquid), because every now and then the volcano awakens and throws acid up as high as 1,900 feet into the air. In the photograph two volcanologists from the Vulcan team are navigating the lake for the first time, in a rubber boat, in order to sample its content at various levels.

2) The two crater lakes of Keli-mutu (Flores, Indonesia) are even more astonishing. The one in the background is rich in sulphuric acid and in greenish iron salts, which give it a turquoise color. The lake in the foreground, which connects with the other, is not acid, but is filled with a dark-red liquid. When the greenish iron salts penetrate the red lake they are destabilized and, in contact with the oxygen of the air, oxidize into reddish iron salts. The resulting color is like the dregs of wine.

1

When two giants clash: eruption versus erosion

Volcanoes are great builders. Within a few thousand years they can modify the topography of a given terrain. To a considerable degree the rising volcanoes of Auvergne (France) disrupted the region, elevating it perceptibly and transforming it into a great water tower, with obvious benefits to agriculture. Also as a result, lakes were formed in the craters and in certain valleys barricaded by the lava flow, as at Aydat, southwest of the city of Clermont-Ferrand.

In East Africa and South America gigantic volcanoes, whose summits lie well within the altitude of perpetual snow, constitute reservoirs for the surrounding region.

1) When the outpouring of lava is especially abundant it may block a bay or cut off an inlet, transforming it

into a lake saturated with salt. This is true of Lake Assal (Djibouti), which is separated from the sea by the volcanic activity of 28,000 years in the south of Afar.

Here there is an endless struggle. As volcanoes build, erosion inexorably destroys, undermines, and eventually levels those volcanic constructions. When Surtsey was born in the ocean south of Iceland in 1963, a titanic struggle between fire and water ensued. The island appeared, was

obliterated by the surge of the waves, rose up again, and again was submerged until, finally, volcanic forces triumphed, building up a permanent structure strong enough to withstand the destructive fury of the Atlantic Ocean. Nevertheless, by degrees, the ocean took its revenge upon the monster. A year after its consolidation, Surtsey's lava flows were already gashed by cliffs cut into the rocks by the waves. Thousands of such islands have had an ephemeral existence be-

fore they were obliterated and consigned to memory.

2) The waterfall of Ofaerafoss (Iceland) has carved out the northwest lip of the largest eruptive fissure of our planet, that of Eldgjā, which came into existence a mere two thousand years ago.

1

The world's saltiest lake

Lake Assal (Djibouti), whose surface is some 500 feet below sea level, is the lowest point in Africa and the saltiest body of water in the world, containing $\frac{7}{10}$ of a pound to every quart of water—that is, ten times the salt content of seawater.

1) With an area of 33 square miles and an average depth of 65 feet, this lake occupies a volcanic depression. It is bordered on the north by salt flats and on the south by an impressive range of basalt mountains. Along the edge is a fantastic chain of halite and gypsum crystals.

2) Here and there magnificent salt atolls stud the blue surface. Ten thousand years ago the lake was situated 260 feet above sea level. A light band in the background of the photograph shows its position at this earlier time. Little by little the dry, hot climate lowered the level, and evaporation made for an increasingly higher proportion of salt to water, thus creating the salt flats mentioned above. At present the level holds. Evaporation (10 cubic meters of water per second) is compensated by the inflow from surrounding wadis and saline springs.

2

3

3) There is no animal life in the brine, but to the southwest, in a hot spring carpeted with green algae, there lives a curious fish, the aphanius, which, due to its extraordinary adaptability, evolved in water with a temperature of 41–45 °C.

A gigantic geode

Lake Assal and its salt flats (Djibouti), together, cover an area of 60 square miles, the world's third-largest area below sea level. They constitute also, the largest geode on the planet, by reason of the deposit of billions of honey-colored gypsum rods and sparkling white cubes of halite, or rock salt.

1) Gypsum crystals can be as long as 6 inches and form amazing mineral flower clusters.

2) Crystals of rock salt attach themselves to branches of gypsum.

3) Along the lake shore salt cubes are broken up by the waves and rolled over and over until they become small transparent balls.

4) Here and there the salt ejects fragments shaped like hollow mushrooms.

Shapes from an extraordinary garden of petrified flowers, where vegetable is mineral . . .

But there is more to the salt of Lake Assal than its poetic beauty. The Bedouins exploit and sell salt as far away as Tibesti and Lake Chad.

5) The Mediterranean dried up six million years ago, when the Strait of Gibraltar was temporarily blocked. It was, at that time, an enormous depressed desert, 9,800 feet below the level of the Atlantic, and must have looked somewhat like the salt flats of Lake Assal. As for the saltiness of the sea, it is produced principally by the hydrothermal activity of underwater volcanic fumaroles, which extracts sodium, chloride, bromides, and iodide from lava and dissolves them in the water.

4

5

Vulcan's treasures: from diamonds to pink flamingos

The process of mineralization associated with volcanism is varied and often has an important economic side. Diamonds stud a rare type of basalt, known as kimberlite, which lines some volcanic chimneys. Kimberlite rocks form at a depth of 125 to 180 miles underground, where temperature and pressure are sufficient to develop diamonds. Eventually these rocks rise in the chimneys, like a fluid rich in gas, and sometimes pierce the earth's surface, touching off a gaseous explosion. Kimberlite chimneys are great upside-down funnels which allow for the extraction of rock samples which otherwise would be inaccessible.

1) From the diamond-bearing chimneys of Kimberley (South Africa) man extracts every year 12 million tons of kimberlite, which is crushed, calibrated, and otherwise treated in such a way as to permit the extraction of its marrow: 2 million carats, that is 4 tons, of diamonds. At Koffiefontein the extraction is often effected in the open air. The largest monocrystal in the world—3,106 carats—was discovered in South Africa's Premier mine in 1905.

2) Lake Magadi (Kenya), whose name comes from the Masai-language word for "bitter," is another example of the fabulous treasure sometimes produced by volcanoes.

Here, in a 100-mile-long hollow, along the Great Rift of Africa, millions of tons of natron have accumulated. This sodium carbonate is percolated out of the surrounding volcanoes by mountain streams or by the alkaline hot springs which rise up into the bottom of the lake. Every year a coating of natron, 4 inches thick, is deposited more than the Magadi Soda Company can refine for sale to glass, soap, textile and paper manufacturers. The rose, vermilion, scarlet, rust, purple, and coral tints of this giant checkerboard are due to algae rich in red canthaxanthine. If flamingos are pink it is because they were raised on this algae, which flourishes only in lakes where there is an abundance of natron. Zoo flamingos turn white if canthaxanthine is not added to their diet.

1

2

1

Forests of peaks and fairy chimneys

These two types of pinnacle, or turret-like, constructions are very similar, but they have quite different origins.

1) Clusters of calcified limestone peaks, lined up over a fault, some of them as high as 210 feet, border the east bank of Lake Abhé (Djibouti), which is heavily loaded with soda. Actually, they are hollow chimneys, some of them still exhaling sulphurous vapor. They formed under water some thousands of years ago, when the level of the lake was considerably higher. Gases and hot-water springs rich in calcium escaped from fractures on the lake bottom, precipitating limestone which formed these gradually emerging structures.

2) These fairy chimneys on the border of the crater lake of Telega Bodas (Java, Indonesia) are the products of erosion. Here they seem to be much larger than they are; their actual height never reaches more than a few feet. Fine clay and pebbly sand were deposited on a flat surface around the edge of the crater. Subsequently rains hollowed the soft matter but could not erode the clay and pebbles, which covered it like an umbrella. This accounts for the formation of these chimneys, each one topped by a protective stone.

1

Volcanoes: great benefactors

The fall of ash produced by an explosive eruption leaves in its wake desolation and sometimes death. But such obvious damage, usually confined to a relatively small area, pales when one considers the benefits which volcanoes have brought to numerous parts of the globe. Sections of Indonesia, Central America, Mexico, the areas surrounding Rome, Naples and Catania (Sicily), Limagne, the plain adjacent to the Massif Central of Auvergne (France), and innumerable other places owe their fertility to volcanic activity.

If Java is Earth's most fertile island, volcanoes deserve the credit. Tropical rains may wash the soil, depriving it of mineral salts, but it is regularly replenished by the fall of volcanic ash, rich in calcium, potassium, and phosphorus. In this hot, damp climate these form a fertilizer falling from the skies. Agronomists have noticed that the more frequent the eruptions of a Javanese volcano, the more

dense the population, since the soil is more fertile. The volcanoes of Java kill some 200 people a year, but their fertility supports 80 million people. Tungurahua (Ecuador) is another example. The 26 million cubic meters of ash which this volcano emitted during its 1916 eruption deposited on the surrounding land nearly 900 pounds of calcium and 88 pounds of potassium per acre.

1) The pumice from the 1912 eruption of Katmai (Alaska) crushed entire forests, but the following year vegetation had already begun to grow up through the layers of ash, except along the Ukak River, where the trees had been submerged in a thick mud flow. Around 1920, when botanists made cuttings from tree trunks which had survived the eruption, they were amazed to find that the growth rings were five times thicker in the years following 1913, years in which the trees had been fertilized by the volcanic ash.

2) The small volcanic island of Augustine (Alaska) underwent a major eruption in 1976 (see pp. 66–67). The volcano was covered with a carpet of ash and pumice, but two years later its slopes were carpeted anew with flowers.

The little prince of sulphur

1) The best description of volcanoes is the one in Saint-Exupéry's *The Little Prince*, which we dedicate to this young carrier of sulphur from the crater of Kawah Idjen (Java, Indonesia): "On the morning of the day of departure he put his planet into good order. He carefully swept the active volcanoes, of which he had two, which were very convenient for cooking an early breakfast. He owned, also, an extinguished volcano. As he always said, 'You never can tell,' and so he swept the extinguished volcano along with the others. Volcanoes, if they are properly swept, burn with a steady, low flame and are not subject to eruption. Eruptions are like chimney fires. Obviously, on our planet, we are too small to properly sweep our volcanoes. That's why they give us so much trouble."

2 and 3) Liquid and crystallized sulphur around the fumaroles of Kawah Idjen.

An angry awakening . . .

Asleep for 123 years, Washington's Mount St. Helens, early on a Sunday morning and almost without warning, literally blew its top, cropping its symmetrical snow-capped cone instantly to a point 1,300 feet lower, shooting hot ash, rock particles and steam some 60,000 feet skyward, denuding hundreds of square miles of surrounding forest, flooding out roads and bridges, choking rivers and harbors with debris washed down the hillsides in rivers of mud, and igniting fires during its brief but unbridled rampage.

Lying 40 miles northeast of Portland, Oregon, in an area of relatively low population, Mount St. Helens nevertheless managed to vomit between one and two cubic miles of its molten insides over an area of some 150 square miles, and propelled a huge cloud of ash eastward that turned day into night in places, forced many people to don breathing masks, and eventually reached the East Coast and beyond.

Not one of the most powerful eruptions on record, the magnitude of the Mount St. Helens blast nevertheless has been likened to that of Mount Vesuvius in A.D. 79, which buried Pompeii, Herculaneum, and Stabiae. Although the loss of human life was much less in the Mount St. Helens disaster (100 or so against 2,000), property damage was in the billions.

1) The terrifying power contained within the earth's crust is dramatically captured in this awesome shot of Mount St. Helens in full eruption on that fatal Sunday morning. The aftermath of the explosion is captured in the three pictures on the right.

2) A man hurriedly attempts to rescue belongings from a house half submerged in mud.

3) Except for the mask, one would think this man were shoveling snow, not hot ash, from his roadway.

4) A timbered mountainside leveled as if by a reaper's scythe.

Index